DR. JEKYLL & MR. HYDE

by

Georg Osterman

SAMUEL FRENCH, INC.
45 WEST 25TH STREET   NEW YORK 10010
7623 SUNSET BOULEVARD HOLLYWOOD 90046
LONDON   TORONTO

Copyright © 1990 by Georg Osterman

ALL RIGHTS RESERVED

CAUTION: Professionals and amateurs are hereby warned that DR. JEKYLL & MR. HYDE is subject to a royalty. It is fully protected under the copyright laws of the United States of America, the British Commonwealth, including Canada, and all other countries of the Copyright Union. All rights, including professional, amateur, motion pictures, recitation, lecturing, public reading, radio broadcasting, television, and the rights of translation into foreign languages are strictly reserved. In its present form the play is dedicated to the reading public only.

The amateur live stage performance rights to DR. JEKYLL & MR. HYDE are controlled exclusively by Samuel French, Inc., and royalty arrangements and licenses must be secured well in advance of presentation. PLEASE NOTE that amateur royalty fees are set upon application in accordance with your producing circumstances. When applying for a royalty quotation and license please give us the number of performances intended, dates of production, your seating capacity and admission fee. Royalties are payable one week before the opening performance of the play to Samuel French, Inc., at 45 W. 25th Street, New York, NY 10010; or at 7623 Sunset Blvd., Hollywood, CA 90046, or to Samuel French (Canada), Ltd., 80 Richmond Street East, Toronto, Ontario, Canada M5C 1P1.

Royalty of the required amount must be paid whether the play is presented for charity or gain and whether or not admission is charged.

Stock royalty quoted on application to Samuel French, Inc.

For all other rights than those stipulated above, apply to Walter Gidaly, Esq., Moldover, Presnick & Gidaly, 750 Third Avenue, New York, NY 10017.

Particular emphasis is laid on the question of amateur or professional readings, permission and terms for which must be secured in writing from Samuel French, Inc.

Copying from this book in whole or in part is strictly forbidden by law, and the right of performance is not transferable.

Whenever the play is produced the following notice must appear on all programs, printing and advertising for the play: "Produced by special arrangement with Samuel French, Inc."

Due authorship credit must be given on all programs, printing and advertising for the play.

ISBN 0 573 69196-7   Printed in U.S.A.

No one shall commit or authorize any act or omission by which the copyright of, or the right to copyright, this play may be impaired.

No one shall make any changes in this play for the purpose of production.

Publication of this play does not imply availability for performance. Both amateurs and professionals considering a production are *strongly* advised in their own interests to apply to Samuel French, Inc., for written permission before starting rehearsals, advertising, or booking a theatre.

No part of this book may be reproduced, stored in a retrieval system, or transmitted in any form, by any means, now known or yet to be invented, including mechanical, electronic, photocopying, recording, videotaping, or otherwise, without the prior written permission of the publisher.

IMPORTANT BILLING AND CREDIT REQUIREMENTS

All producers of DR. JEKYLL & MR. HYDE *must* give credit to the Author of the Play in all programs distributed in connection with performances of the Play and in all instances in which the title of the Play appears for purposes of advertising, publicizing or otherwise exploiting the Play and/or a production. The name of the Author *must* also appear on a separate line, on which no other name appears, immediately following the title, and *must* appear in size of type not less than fifty percent the size of the title type.

The following must also appear in all programs in connection with a performance:

"Originally Produced by THE RIDICULOUS THEATRICAL COMPANY of New York City"

Dr. Jekyll and Mr. Hyde was originally produced November, 1989, in New York City by The Ridiculous Theatrical Company.

Cast in order of appearance was:

MINERVA	Terence Mintern
MARY JEKYLL	Eureka
HENRY JEKYLL	Everett Quinton
BERNICE BRAINTWAIN	Mary Neufeld
LILY GAY	Georg Osterman
ACULINE	Minnette Coleman

Costumes by Susan Young
Scenery by Mark Beard
Lighting by Richard Currie
Directed by Kate Stafford

CHARACTERS

MINERVA	The Jekyll's maid. A tough cookie.
MARY JEKYLL	Henry's wife. A little on the dizzy side.
DR. HENRY JEKYLL	A brilliant scientist and devoted husband.
DR. BERNICE BRAINTWAIN	Henry's associate and close friend.
LILY GAY	A pretty night club singer/opera instructor.
ACULINE	A beautiful black night club owner. Bernice's lover.
EDDIE HYDE	The wickedest man in all Coxsackie. A real sleaze-bag.
JEHOVAH'S WITNESS	An innocent bystander/fire-and-brimstone spouter.
COCO	A caged monkey in Henry's lab.

ACT I

Scene 1

SCENE: The Jekyll home. The TELEPHONE rings. MINERVA, the Jekylls' maid, enters.

MINERVA. I'll get it! (*SHE picks up the receiver.*) The Jekyll residence ... No, I'm sorry, the Doctor isn't in. Would you like to leave a message? ... Rudimentary Aphasia. Could you please spell that? ... R-U-D ... Hello. Hello? ... This is the Jekyll residence ... No. I didn't call you. You called me ... No, I don't know why you're calling ... Rudimentary something-or-other, I don't remember ... Oh. You don't remember either? ... Well, I'll have the doctor get back to you as soon as he comes in. What's you name, hon? ...Well, is it written down somewhere? Check your mail ... You don't know if that's your home? ... Look, Sweetie. Why don't you try calling him at the institute ... Yes ... okay, you got a pencil? That's the Coxsackie Medical Institute ... 716-5000, extension 666, the neurophysics department ... Neu-ro-phys-ics ... Look ... Why don't you just call the Institute and ask for Dr. Jekyll ... Dr. Jekyll! ... right ... right ... okay ... Goodbye.

(*SHE hangs up the phone and takes a deep breath as MARY JEKYLL enters carrying a matchbook and an envelope.*)

MARY. Minerva, who was that?
MINERVA. I don't know, Mrs. J.

MARY. Oh. Would you bring me a stamp? (*Filling out the inside of the matchbook.*) I'm so excited! I'm going to take up opera.

MINERVA. Oh, boy.

(*MARY hands her the matchbook and SHE reads aloud.*)

MINERVA. Yes, I want to be an opera singer regardless of my experience. I would like to enroll as a check one: soprano, alto, mezzo soprano, contralto, tenor, counter tenor, baritone, bass. Send me ten trial lessons for only nineteen, ninety-five, not including shipping and handling ... blah, blah, blah ... Send check or money order to: Coxsackie Correspondence Conservatory ... Do not mail matches.

MARY. (*Takes back the matches.*) I'll receive one lesson a week for ten weeks, *and* if I enroll today I'll also receive, free-of-charge, a custom-designed tape player available only through this offer. (*Stamps the envelope.*)

MINERVA. And how long will this last?

MARY. What do you mean, Minerva?

MINERVA. When I think of all the courses you've taken through the mail. ... What about that "Become a Psychic in 30 days"?

MARY. I've never told anyone this, but I did become very sensitive to peoples' innermost thoughts, and I'll tell you, Minerva, it was a bottomless pit. I had to give it up for the sake of my own sanity.

MINERVA. Well, what about that Modern Utopia Series? "Cooking With Algae"? "Communal Living Through Computer Interface"?

MARY. Urban anthropology just wasn't my cup of tea.

MINERVA. And that last one ...Making anti-personal devices out of common household items. Half the light bulbs in the house were filled with gunpowder. Walking

DR. JEKYLL & MR. HYDE   9

through the drawing room was like navigating a mine field. You nearly killed one of Dr. Jekyll's patients with the nitro-guanidine doorknob.

MARY. (*Proud.*) Ah, my first kitchen-improvised blasting cap. I had a true interest in that ... and I was very good at it, I might add. But Henry put his foot down. He said it was futile, his trying to save lives when I was trying to destroy them. Do you believe it? He actually raised his voice to me when Mr. Sanchez opened the door and the knob exploded in his hand. Oh, he was more frightened than injured. I don't see why Henry got so angry.

MINERVA. Another man would have divorced you. I've never met a man as mild and even tempered as Doctor Jekyll.

MARY. He is wonderful, isn't he?

MINERVA. And so hard working.

MARY. Yes, the poor dear. He had another emergency last night. He's hardly slept a wink. When he comes in I want him to go straight to bed.

(*A CRASH of glass is heard.*)

MINERVA. There's the paper. (*Exits, then shouts off ...*) Good shot, Mortimer. (*Reenters reading the* Coxsackie Tatler.) Good God! Listen to this. "Secret Psycho Seized." There's a psycho in Coxsackie.

MARY. What's news about that? The *Coxsackie Tatler* has become such a tabloid.

MINERVA. Listen. (*Reads.*) Basil Hickock, a seemingly mild-mannered librarian ...

MARY. Basil Hickock? What about Basil Hickock?

MINERVA. Well, let me read the article. (*Continues reading.*) ... mild-mannered librarian ... was caught late last night in the act of dismembering the dead body of his 68-

year-old mother, Mrs. Hattie Hickock of 1185 Winona Boulevard, Coxsackie.

MARY. I never much cared for that woman.

MINERVA. (*Reads.*) "Police Officer Mitch Patterson stumbled upon the grisly crime while on a routine neighborhood patrol at 11:30 pm Thursday. Officer Patterson stated that he knocked on the Hickock door to inform the residents that the headlights were left on in the car parked out front. Patterson became suspicious when Hickock answered the door covered with blood. When questioned, Hickock insisted he'd cut himself shaving, and became violent when Patterson asked to, quote, take a look around, unquote. Gaining entry to the house, he discovered the scattered remains of Mrs. Hickock in the living room, kitchen, and dining room. Further investigation revealed a horrifying collection of other human remains. The refrigerator was filled with human organs, and a large freezer in the cellar was packed with butchered parts. The county coroner's office has numbered the total body count at 16 and a half. When Officer Patterson returned to the living room to make a formal arrest, he found Hickock sitting calmly in a chair, apparently unaware of what had just transpired. Hickock was arrested, arraigned and remanded to the care of the Coxsackie Correctional Institute for the Criminally Insane until he is able to stand trial."

(*SOUND of car door slamming.*)

MARY. Little Basil Hickock. I remember when *he* was the paper boy. *He* had better aim. It just goes to show, Minerva, you never can tell.

(*HENRY JEKYLL enters.*)

MARY. Henry, look at you. You must be exhausted.

HENRY. I'm a little tired, that's all. Good morning, Mary. (*Gives Mary a peck on the cheek.*)
MARY. Goodnight, Henry.
HENRY. I can't sleep now. I'm expecting Dr. Braintwain.
MARY. Can't this wait?

(*As HENRY walks toward his laboratory door MINERVA grabs hold of his suit jacket and pulls it off in one fell swoop.*)

HENRY. Good morning, Minerva.
MINERVA. Morning, Doctor J. (*Exits.*)
MARY. I'm terribly worried about you, Henry. You haven't had a decent night's sleep for a week. You work all day then come home and putter about in that laboratory of yours till all hours of the night ... And didn't you just leave Dr. Braintwain at the Institute? Why is she coming here?
HENRY. She's bringing someone here I really must speak with. We had an extraordinary case last night and Bernice has managed to locate a friend of the patient's who may be able to shed some light on the incidents that triggered his disorder. It may be too early to say, but it looks like a classic example of Quantum Synaptic Dualism.
MARY. Will Braintwain be able to revive you when you completely collapse from exhaustion?

(*The DOORBELL rings. MINERVA enters and answers it.*)

HENRY. That must be her now.

(*BERNICE BRAINTWAIN enters.*)

BERNICE. Thanks Minerva. Is Dr. Jekyll ... Oh, there you are, Henry. Good morning, Mary.
MARY. If your husband was dying from exhaustion, you wouldn't think it was so good. (*SHE exits.*)

(*MINERVA brings in a tray with coffee.*)

HENRY. You'll have to excuse Mary. After all these years she still hasn't gotten used to ...
BERNICE. Being a doctor's wife?

(*HENRY shakes his head "yes." MINERVA stands by closely to listen.*)

BERNICE. I understand ... Look ... I met Hickock's girl friend. She's rather exotic.
HENRY. That will be *all*, Minerva.

(*MINERVA rolls her eyes and exits.*)

HENRY. Where is this girl friend?
BERNICE. She'll be along shortly.
HENRY. Would you like some coffee?
BERNICE. Great.

(*HENRY gives her a cup.*)

BERNICE. Thanks.
HENRY. I don't suppose you heard anything from the board of trustees?
BERNICE. Actually, Henry ... your proposal hasn't been submitted to the board yet.
HENRY. But I put it on your desk last week.

BERNICE. And I read it. Surely you're not serious about this transmutation business?

HENRY. I *am* serious! Dead serious! This is my life's work! You have no right to withhold it from the board.

BERNICE. I have *every* right! Do you honestly think the board is going to allocate money for you to waste?

(*MINERVA peeks in unnoticed to eavesdrop.*)

HENRY. Waste?!! This is a very important experiment, Bernice.

BERNICE. Turning gold into base metal? You call that an important experiment? I call it balderdash. Utter nonsense ... You'll be a laughing stock. I won't stand by and watch the reputation of the entire department go down with you.

(*MINERVA exits quietly.*)

HENRY. It was seven years ago on *your* recommendation, Bernice, that I was brought to the Institute. You believed in me then, and my experiments linking particle decay with neurological disorders put The Coxsackie Medical Institute on the map. Back then the neurophysics department consisted of two scientists and a lab geek who were using Baryon Lepton Fusion to treat nominal schizophrenia, a breakthrough procedure you perfected, Doctor, but one that was not an end in itself. What you discovered was the key, but the key is no good without a lock. *I* discovered the lock. On the basis of *my* work, the department came up with a metaphysical approach to the brain. I refer of course to the neurological equivalent of the Unified Field Theory: Particle Education. The atoms of the brain had simply to be convinced of the moral necessity of coherent molecular behavior. You scoffed at my theory, but it brought results. And results, my dear Dr. Braintwain, are what science is all about.

BERNICE. I realize your past accomplishments. A philosophical approach to science has often been of value ... Darwin, Jung, Helsenberg ... But philosophy is not magic. Alchemy *is*. I have nothing against magic as entertainment, but I question its medical application.

HENRY. You'd be more interested in my experiment if it promised to bring in a healthy endowment from the board of trustees.

BERNICE. Ouch! ... Now hold hon, Henry...

(*The DOORBELL rings.*)

BERNICE. That must be Hickock's girl friend. We'll discuss this further some other time.

(*SHE answers the door. LILY GAY enters.*)

BERNICE. Miss Gay, it's very good of you to come. This is Dr. Jekyll. Doctor, this is Miss Lily Gay.

LILY. Nice place you got here, Doc.

HENRY. Thank you, Miss Gay.

LILY. Lily.

HENRY. Lily ... Coffee?

LILY. No thanks. The stuff makes me nuts. Now what can I do to you ... I mean *for* you?

BERNICE. We need your help, Lily.

LILY. Miss Gay.

BERNICE. I think I'll leave you to Dr. Jekyll, Miss Gay. He's in charge. I'll check in on the patient, Henry. You *will* call me this afternoon?

HENRY. Of course, Doctor.

BERNICE. Miss Gay.

LILY. Yeah. Yeah ...

DR. JEKYLL & MR. HYDE

(BERNICE exits. LILY pounces on Henry.)

LILY. So what's you pleasure, Doc?
HENRY. Miss Gay!!!
LILY. Lily.
HENRY. Lily! I need your help.
LILY. Well, what do ya think I'm tryin' ta give ya?
HENRY. Not *that* kind of help!
LILY. Suit yourself, Doc. I can get into *any* scene.
HENRY. Just what did Doctor Braintwain say to you?
LILY. That there was a doctor friend of hers that she wanted me to see ... I don't mind doin' a little *overtime* so here I am.
HENRY. Then you haven't heard about Basil Hickock?
LILY. What about him? Wait! Before you go any further ... I've only know him five or six months ... hardly know him at all. He drank hard, played hard, and always had money. I never asked how he got it. He was good to me and I was *very* good to him. That's *it*. Now, what's all the fuss, Doc? Is he hurt or somethin'?
HENRY. Lily, Bernice ... Doctor Braintwain, got your name from his wallet ...
LILY. He's dead?
HENRY. No, no. Please have a seat.

(SHE sits.)

HENRY. Lily, Basil is in trouble.
LILY. So what's new? What was it, another fight? He's always fighting. Look! I don't want to have anything to do with this. I have my career to think of.
HENRY. There is evidence that Basil Hickock brutally murdered fifteen people over the past few months. He was

caught last night in the act of dismembering his sixteenth victim ... his mother.

LILY. You mean the whole time he was seeing me ...

HENRY. You're a very lucky woman, Lily.

LILY. Lucky? I've always been lucky. I sure can pick 'em. I must have a built-in divining rod for trouble.

HENRY. What do you mean?

LILY. It started with Louie.

HENRY. Where is this Louie?

LILY. In the slammer. The Coxsackie Correctional Institute for the Criminally Insane.

HENRY. What's Louie in for?

LILY. Murder.

HENRY. Murder?

LILY. That's what I said. You see, Louie was a lunger by trade.

HENRY. A lunger?

LILY. One of the best.

HENRY. What's a lunger?

LILY. It was his job to remove the lungs from the chickens in the packin' plant in Buffalo. It's a very specialized field, lunging. Well Louie had this boss who didn't appreciate his special talents. He was always brow-beatin' him. Well, one day Louie just snapped. He lunged the boss right there in the special parts section.

HENRY. Remarkable! His co-workers witnessed the grisly incident?

LILY. Along with a couple thousand chickens on death row.

HENRY. I seem to remember this case ... yes, Louie the Lunger. Braintwain handled the case herself. Simple Dissociative Reaction ... So you followed this Louie the Lunger here to Coxsackie?

LILY. What else would a girl like me be doin' in a dumpy burg like this?

HENRY. Have there been other men?

LILY. Sure. I've tried on other men for size. That's how I met Basil. Talk about lucky. Well, if you'll excuse me, Doc. (*Gets up to leave.*)

HENRY. (*Stops her.*) Where are you going?

LILY. Home. This is trouble with a capital "T." If the cops come, I have to talk to them, but there's no law that says I have to talk to you.

HENRY. Please, Lily. You must help us. The man you described is nothing like the Basil Hickock known to the community. Everybody knows Basil. He's a sweet, harmless librarian. You're the only person alive who knows the *other* Basil Hickock, the psychopath capable of committing these heinous atrocities.

LILY. I get it. You need *me* to cop an insanity plea. Well, forget it! This is crazy.

HENRY. Basil Hickock is not crazy. He's suffering from a rare disorder I discovered known as Quantum Synaptic Dualism. A disease wherein two distinct and rational beings inhabit the same body.

LILY. Rational? You think it's rational to kill ... what was it ... sixteen people?

HENRY. In this case, yes. It's a form of split-brain syndrome. In a brain afflicted with Quantum Synaptic Dualism two separate moralities exist. For Basil Hickock killing *is* a rational act. It's his evil half expressing itself. Is that clear? Any questions?

LILY. Is it sexually transmitted?

HENRY. No. No. It has to do with the electro-chemical activity in the brain. In my opinion it's triggered by over-stimulation of the hypothalamus.

LILY. Don't look at me. I never touched his hypothalamus.

HENRY. Well, you might have, indirectly. Did he ever achieve a state of overwhelming sexual excitement during the time you've known him?

LILY. Doc, I'm good, but I ain't *that* good. Basil was never a winner in the funsy-wunsy department. He just wanted me to take freezing cold showers then lay there like I was dead while he drew little patterns with a butter knife all over my naked body. Would you call *that* overwhelming?

HENRY. That's it! That explains it! The dead bodies ...

LILY. What are you saying, Doc?

HENRY. Basil was playing a game with you, Lily. Tracing out his plans. But it was no game for those sixteen other people.

LILY. Oh, my God! You mean I *did* have something to do with it?!

HENRY. No, Lily. You were just as much a victim ... well, not *just* as much ... in any case, you bear no responsibility for the heinous crimes committed by Basil Hickock. Clear your conscience of this whole matter ... I want to thank you, Lily. You've been a great help whether you realize it or not. (*Takes out a calling card and hands it to her.*) If I can ever be of any help to you, please feel free to call on me.

LILY. (*Looks at the card.*) While I'm here ... there *is* something you can help me with.

HENRY. Yes?

LILY. (*Stands close to him and points to her throat.*) Well, Doc. I get these sharp pains right here.

HENRY. (*Innocently feels.*) Here?

LILY. Yeah. And then they move down to *here*. (*SHE grabs his hand and plants it on her breast.*)

HENRY. (*Catching on.*) I see.

LILY. Ooooh, then I get these other pains right here. (*SHE moves his hand around her waist and THEY begin to struggle.*)
LILY. Miss Gay!!!
LILY. Lily!
HENRY. Lily, I'm a happily married man.
LILY. Some of my best friends are happily married men. Come on, Doc. Opperate!!!

(*Wrestling, THEY fall into an armchair as MINERVA enters.*)

MINERVA. Oooohhh!!! Excuse me! (*Flustered, SHE begins to exit.*)
HENRY. (*Leaping up.*) Minerva! Wait! I ... I'd like to introduce you to Miss Lily Gay. She's been helping me with an important case.
LILY. Pleased to make your acquaintance.
MINERVA. (*Glaring.*) I'm sure!
LILY. Well, Doctor Jekyll, I'm glad I could be of some service, but I really must run. This is late for me. Got to get my beauty sleep. I work nights at a place called "The Fruit Bowl." If you're ever in the neighborhood, drop in. (*To Minerva.*) Oh, you too, of course.

(*MINERVA gives her a look that could melt stone.*)

HENRY. Thank you once again. Minerva, will you show Miss Gay out?
MINERVA. Delighted.
LILY. Goodbye, Doctor.
HENRY. Miss Gay.

(*LILY mouths the word "Lily," before MINERVA hustles her out. HENRY looks befuddled. MINERVA returns.*)

HENRY. Minerva ...

MINERVA. There's no need to say anything, Doctor Jekyll. I'm sure it was all perfectly innocent. You certainly don't own *me* an explanation. This is your home and you're free to do as you please. It's not *my* place to judge other people's indiscretions. Far be it from me to point the finger at anyone. God knows to err is human. I've certainly made *my* share of mistakes. There's no need to worry. (*SHE begins to sniffle.*) Mrs. Jekyll doesn't have to hear a word this. Why it would break her heart. There's enough pain in the world. (*SHE breaks down sobbing.*)

HENRY. (*Comforting her.*) There, there, Minerva. You're being so silly. Stop crying. Nothing happened.

MINERVA. (*Weeping with her head on his shoulder.*) You don't have to explain anything to me. I know how it is. I've been there myself.

(*MARY JEKYLL enters.*)

MINERVA. But Mrs. Jekyll would never understand. Mrs. Jekyll!!!

MARY. There's no need to say anything, Minerva. I'm sure it's all perfectly innocent. Now, Henry. Your guests are gone. To bed!

HENRY. Mary, you're a dear. I'll be in my laboratory. Please don't disturb me unless it's of the utmost importance. (*HE exits into this laboratory.*)

MINERVA. (*Disappointed.*) Oh, Henry!

(*SHE shakes her head as MINERVA shrugs her shoulders. LIGHTS out.*)

ACT I

Scene 2

SCENE: The laboratory of Dr. Henry Jekyll later that day. It is very industrial and clean with a chemistry set-up, etc. there is a caged monkey named Coco against one wall. HENRY, wearing a crisp white lab coat, is muttering mathematical equations and writing them on a blackboard.

HENRY. If $P=-Q$ then $2\pi \times \sqrt{-1} > P+-Q \times HN$ ... NO, no, no, no , no.... (*Erases the board.*) Patience, Henry Jekyll. Rome wasn't built in a day. (*Goes to the computer and begins typing.*) Of course, turning gold into base metal is of secondary importance. I'm working by analogy, any fool can see that. But an educated fool like Dr. Braintwain can't see the innate poetry of science ... the alchemy of chemistry. By devolving gold to its base constituents I hope to achieve a deeper understanding of matter transformation, and so apply it to the molecular structure of the brain. (*Goes to the chemistry set-up and starts pouring things from various vessels into a test tube.*) By seductive induction, I will lure nature backwards to her bare elements. (*As HE pours the next solution from a beaker, the test tube begins to smoke.*) It's changing color! Could it be? A simple salt solution added to the previous ingredients ... I must test this formula at once! (*HE sets the test tube into its stand and unwraps a golden bowl. With a small paint brush, HE coats the bowl with the formula in the tube and sets it on the counter.*) I must record the transmutation. (*HE prepares his tape recorder.*) Testing. Testing. One, two, three ...

(*There is a KNOCK at the door.*)

HENRY. Who is it?
MINERVA. (*Off.*) It's Minerva, Dr. J.
HENRY. What do you want?
MINERVA. Mrs. J had me make you up a little lunch.
HENRY. Go away, Minerva. I'm not hungry.
MINERVA. (*Very butch.*) The Mrs. says if you don't eat something she's gonna come in there and force-feed you herself.
HENRY. (*Under his breath, worried.*) Mary can't come in here. She'll see the bowl.

(*HE opens the door and lets MINERVA in. SHE carries a tray laden with luncheon items and a pot of coffee.*)

HENRY. Set it down over there, but be very, very, very, very, very, very careful.
MINERVA. Gotcha. (*Sets the tray down on the counter and notices the bowl.*) Doctor! That golden bow is Mrs. J's anniversary gift from her favorite Aunt Zena.
HENRY. It belongs to the both of us. Besides, Zena should have given us tin instead of gold, since it was only our tenth anniversary. (*Aside.*) If this experiment is successful, that oversight will be remedied.
MINERVA. You're *not* going to use that bowl in your silly experiments?
HENRY. Et tu, Minerva?
MINERVA. It's worth a fortune!
HENRY. To me, this experiment's beyond price. Now please, Minerva! I must continue. (*Pushes her toward the door.*)
MINERVA. But ...
HENRY. Please!!!
MINERVA. All right, Doctor. Whatever you say. Ya don't have to shove.

(*SHE exits. HENRY forgot to turn off the tape recorder. HE rewinds and listens. Frustrated HE rewinds entirely and beings recording again as HE looks closely at the bowl.*)

HENRY. 12:35 pm. I have coated the object thoroughly with the formula. As of yet, there is no visible change of color or conversion of any sort ...

(*HE walks away from the bowl and begins to pace back and forth. MINERVA sneaks back in and replaces the golden bowl with an automobile hubcap of the same shape, and exits without HENRY noticing.*)

HENRY. Braintwain claims that Quantum Synaptic Dualism is but Dr. Jekyll's wild *theory*, and that Basil Hickock is suffering from extreme reactive schizophrenia. This would mean there is a separation of the individual from his behavior ... I've examined this man thoroughly. The Basil Hickock I know *is* goodness itself. A man with a heart of pure gold ... But, Miss Lily Gay's Basil *is* evil. His soul is as ugly as corroded pot metal. It's like there are twins living in his body, but only one at a time can they emerge from their separate, darkened rooms to the light of day ... But is it possible to prove this? Is it vanity pure and simple? Am I caught up with the idea of success so much that I've lost all perception of reality? (*HE notices the hubcap.*) My God! It's changed! Not only has a chemical transmutation taken place, but the actual shape has been altered ... Just you wait, Bernice Braintwain! Just you wait! Now if only I could test it on a living being. Theoretically it should work.

(*COCO the monkey screams and jumps about wildly in the cage.*)

HENRY. Don't worry, Coco! I won't try it on.

(*COCO gives a sigh of relief.*)

HENRY. No offense, but the Humane Society's been like a monkey on my back lately ... Braintwain and the Institute would never let me use the formula on Basil, the man I wish to cure. Without their support, what option am I left with? But, do I dare to become my own test rat? It's a chance I'm not afraid to take. Braintwain would call it madness ... If this be madness, I envy no man the world calls sane! (*HE drinks the formula.*) Hmmm ... not bad. But I don't feel a thing.

(*COCO goes crazy again.*)

HENRY. Calm down, Coco!!! Here ... (*HE gives Coco his sandwich.*) You eat this. I'm not hungry. We mustn't let anyone know what's going on in here. It's our little secret, Coco. You got that?

(*COCO makes an affirmative grunt, "uh-huh."*)

HENRY. Damn! Why didn't it work? There must be something missing. (*HE pours a cup of coffee and drinks it down.*) Ach! Minerva, your coffee's getting worse every day ... Ohhhh!!! Ohhhh!!! She's poisoned me!!! (*HE is seized with racking pains. The walls breathe as the room becomes a bizarre hallucination. HENRY gasps wildly for breath as everything SPINS around him. HE appears to be shrinking.*) Lord God! What have I done?!!! I feel my bones grinding!!!

(*Suddenly the pains cease. The spinning stops. HE is transformed from Henry to a smaller, hideous EDWARD HYDE.*)

HYDE. What has caused this inexplicable trauma? (*Looks into the coffee cup.*) Unbelievable! Could it be? Minerva's dreadful coffee is the necessary catalyst! ... This is marvelous! I feel years younger. I've never felt so wonderfully, wickedly alive!!! I must see myself! (*Clears the luncheon tray and uses it as a looking glass.*) Is this my other self? Could I have so evil a side to me? (*Looking closer.*) You are ugly, my friend, but I feel no repugnance. But rather a leap of welcome! I must study you further. (*Notices the tape deck and talks into it.*) Upon taking the formula the most racking pangs succeeded; a grinding of the bones, deadly nausea, and a horror of the spirit that cannot be exceeded at the hour of birth or death. Then these agonies began swiftly to subside, and I came to myself as if out of a great sickness. There is something strange in my sensations, something indescribably new and, from its very novelty, incredibly sweet. I feel younger, lighter, happier in body; within I am conscious of a heady recklessness. Sensual images race through my mind! (*Feels his crotch.*) I believe I've lost in stature ... The bonds of obligation are gone! I feel an innocent freedom of the soul!!!

(*There is a KNOCK at the door.*)

HENRY. Who is it?
MINERVA. (*Off.*) Henry? Who's in there with you?
HENRY. Nobody! (*Spots a lab frog and begins to eat it alive.*) I've got a frog in my throat.

MINERVA. Henry, come out of there at once or I'm coming in. I won't stand by and let you work yourself into some terrible state.

HYDE. No! I ... I'll be out in a minute. Just let me finish what I'm doing.

MINERVA. All right, Henry. I'll give you five minutes.

HENRY. I must further investigate this phenomenon before allowing anyone to know of its discovery. I must hide all evidence ... (*Begins putting everything away.*) ... hide all evidence ... Hide ... Mr. Hyde ... I christen you, My newfound friend. Mr. Hyde! We'll meet again ... this evening. (*HE toasts himself with the coffee cup and laughs maniacally as the LIGHTS fade out.*)

ACT I

Scene 3

SCENE: The Fruit Bowl, late that same evening. Upstage there is a small platform with a microphone. Downstage there are a couple of small tables with chairs that comprise the club. Everything looks slightly seedy. EDWARD HYDE sits at one of the tables drinking alone. ACULINE, the hostess and owner of the club, takes the stage. APPLAUSE. SHE is a beautiful black woman.

ACULINE. (*Into the microphone.*) Thank you and welcome. I guess most of you know me ... (*Cat calls.*)

That's right, Honey. For those of you who don't ... I'm Miss Aculine. (*APPLAUSE*.) Thank you. Wow! What a pretty bunch. Bunch of *what* I won't say .. but you sure are pret-tay ... (*SHE spots Hyde*.) Woops! Spoke too soon ... Ooo-ooo, Child! You are ug-ly! I wouldn't kiss that face with a borrowed set of lips. Mmm-mmm. You should have lived in the dark ages with *that* face. Hey, Mister! Is this some kinda sight gag? ... Such a sight, he make me wanna gag! Now seriously ... take off that mask. It ain't Halloween and you're scarin' me ...

(*HYDE glares at her. SHE is shaken.*)

ACULINE. All right ... Let's get on with the show ... Ladies and Ladies ... The Fruit Bowl is *extremely* proud to present our own Miss Coxsackie ... Miss Lily Gay!!! ... And, boy is she ...

(*LILY enters and either sings or lip-synchs a hot torch song or disco number. After APPLAUSE SHE exits. ACULINE goes over to Hyde.*)

ACULINE. Listen, Mister. I was just havin' a little fun with you back there.
HYDE. A little fun with me?
ACULINE. Yeah. No hard feelings?
HYDE. I like hard feelings and I like feeling hard.
ACULINE. Don't we all? What's your name?
HYDE. Edward Hyde.
ACULINE. Hide, huh? How about a drink, Mr. Hyde. It's on me.
HYDE. What a good idea. (*HE splashes her with his drink.*) It's on you.
ACULINE. (*Angry.*) So you're a comedian, huh?!
HYDE. (*Revelation.*) Yes ... a comedian.

ACULINE. Well, tonight's Friday night! Stand-up night's next Thursday. Listen, I probably deserved that. Now, let me get you a drink. What'll it be?

HYDE. Whiskey.

ACULINE. On the rocks? Or if you'll pardon the expression ... straight.

HYDE. Straight.

ACULINE. I kinda thought so. Well, suit yourself, Chief. Comin' right up. (*SHE turns to walk to the bar.*)

HYDE. Cock-suckin' whore!!!

ACULINE. What?!!!

HYDE. I said, "Coxsackie's a bore."

ACULINE. Well, we do what we can. I didn't think you were a local.

HYDE. I'm not a local. I'm an express. Hee hee hee ...

ACULINE. Well, choo-choo, Baby! Save it for stand-up night. (*Calling off.*) Max! Whiskey! Make it a breeder! (*SHE exits.*)

HYDE. My unpremeditated discovery has thrust unforeseen experiences on me ... What a deliciously dreadful dump. Dr. Jekyll would simply abhor it, but Mr. Hyde feels as triumphant as the plague. Think of it ... Edward Hyde, stand-up comedian. Jekyll detests comics. Hee hee hee. We are so different, he and I. He would say diametrical opposites or polar twins, the poor man ...

(*BERNICE BRAINTWAIN enters and sits at the other table.*)

HYDE. Well, if it isn't the good, safe Dr. Braintwain.

(*LILY enters.*)

BERNICE. Lily!

LILY. Hi, hon. (*THEY give each other a friendly peck.*) Say, Bernie. Ya got anymore doctors for me to talk to? That guy this morning...

BERNICE. Doctor Jekyll?

LILY. Yeah. Henry. He's a washout in the romance department, but a cutie just the same.

BERNICE. He's married.

LILY. That's what *he* said.

ACULINE. (*Enters carrying a double straight whiskey.*) Hi, Bernie Baby. (*SHE sets down the drink and falls into a passionate embrace with Bernice.*) Mmmm-mmmm. That's just what I needed a little sugar in my bowl.

LILY. L'amour, l'amour. Tous jour l'amour.

BERNICE. Honey, you smell like you've been bathing in that stuff. (*Indicates the drink.*)

ACULINE. Don't get all bent up, Bernie. That guy over there baptized me with his.

BERNICE. (*Angry.*) With his *what?!* Let met at him!

ACULINE. Bernie! Take a chill pill, Child! I had it comin'. I made a fool outta the sucker and he splashed me with his drink.

BERNICE. Which one is he?

ACULINE. The tough little troll over a table five. Name's Edward Hyde.

LILY. Ugh! He oughta hide. Hey ... he looks like a "Chia Pet."

BERNICE. Well, beauty's only skin deep.

ACULINE. Then somebody oughtta *skin* that sucker ... Lily, would you bring Mr. Sunshine his drink? It's on-the-house.

LILY. Aculine!

ACULINE. Pretty please?

LILY. All riiiight. (*SHE goes over to Hyde with the drink.*) Here's your drink.

HYDE. (*Hands her a twenty dollar bill.*) Thank you, Lily.

LILY. How'd you know my name?

HYDE. I caught your act.

LILY. Lucky you didn't catch anything else. (*Gives him back the twenty.*) You can keep this. The drink's on the house.

HYDE. (*Shoves it down her bra.*) I know. That's your tip.

LILY. Gee. Thanks, Mister ...

HYDE. Edward Hyde ... Will you join me for a moment?

LILY. I suppose I could, Edward.

(*As SHE sits down HE slips his hand under her rump. SHE screams and jumps up falsely scolding him.*)

LILY. How about Eddie?

HYDE. (*Smelling his fingers.*) What?

LILY. Can I call you Eddie? It's a lot easier than Edward.

HYDE. Certainly.

LILY. Good. Well, Eddie ... What brings you to The Fruit Bowl?

HYDE. You, Lily.

LILY. Me?

HYDE. Yes. A mutual friend recommended you and this place.

LILY. I see ... All right, Good Lookin'. What's your pleasure?

HYDE. You think I'm good looking?

LILY. For the right price, every man's good looking.

HYDE. Doctor Jekyll was right. You *are* a wild one.

LILY. You know Henry Jekyll?

HYDE. Yes. We're *very* close.

LILY. Now there's a guy who stays on a girl's mind ... like a heavy meal.

HYDE. What am *I* like?

LILY. Antipasto.

HYDE. Are you attached, Lily?

LILY. (*Checks to see if she's hooked on her chair.*) To what?

HYDE. I meant, do you have a special fellow?

LILY. Why should I tell you? You'd just get all upset. Most men do. They all want to be the only man in a woman's life, no matter how many women they have in theirs.

HYDE. I was just curious.

LILY. Curiosity didn't do much for the cat.

HYDE. Satisfaction did ... and you look like a girl who knows how to satisfy.

LILY. I do. No brag. Just fact.

HYDE. (*Laughs wickedly.*) Ha ha ha ha ha ...

BERNICE. Sounds like Lily's got the little toad goin'.

ACULINE. Goin' where? Bernie, that guy gives me the gay willies. There's somethin' evil about him.

BERNICE. He can't help it if he's ugly. Did it ever occur to you that inside that crude exterior there might be a warm, sensitive human being?

ACULINE. Not unless he ate one ... It's not just that he's ugly, it's something more. God bless me, the man seems hardly human.

BERNICE. Something troglodytic, shall we say?

ACULINE. Say whatever *you* want ... *I* say he's got the signature of Satan on that face.

HYDE. What's your drink, Lily?

LILY. Champagne.

HYDE. Can I buy you some?

LILY. Not here. I think the stuff *they* serve comes in cans. I've got a bottle of "Verve Cliqout" in my fridge at home.

HYDE. Expensive taste.

LILY. I suck it up like a "Hoover Deluxe."

BERNICE. What do you suppose they're talking about?

ACULINE. I don't know, but I'll bet he's got her signin' somethin' in blood by now.

BERNICE. A curious fellow, this Hyde. I'd like to study him more closely.

ACULINE. That's askin' for big trouble, Bernice.

(*LILY gets up and comes over to them.*)

ACULINE. Here comes Lily.

LILY. Aculine, I'm gonna cut out a little early tonight.

ACULINE. With him?

LILY. Yes.

ACULINE. Where you goin'? To the zoo?

LILY. What for?

ACULINE. To visit the rest of his family.

LILY. Don't make fun of Mr. Hyde.

ACULINE. It's his *hide* I'm makin' fun of. Girl, you sure know how to pick 'em.

LILY. Well, for your information, he's got some pretty class friends. He even knows Henry Jekyll, Bernie.

BERNICE. He must be one of Henry's patients.

LILY. I don't think so. He said they're *very* close. How close do you get with *your* patients?

BERNICE. Not very.

ACULINE. (*Shivers.*) I hope not.

HYDE. (*Coming over to join them.*) Are you ready, Lily my dear?

LILY. As ready as I'll ever be.

ACULINE. Ready for what?

DR. JEKYLL & MR. HYDE   33

HYDE. Then we'll bid you both farewell. (*Then to Bernice.*) Funny. All these people around ... (*Indicates audience.*) and no one bothered to introduce us.

BERNICE. (*Puts out her hand to shake his.*) I guess they didn't.

HYDE. (*Pulls away.*) And I'd like to thank each and every one of them ... See you on stand-up night.

BERNICE. Well!

(*LILY and HYDE exit. LIGHTS out.*)

ACT I

Scene 4

SCENE: LILY GAY'S apartment, minutes later. There are wigs, audio-cassette tapes, and sheet music everywhere. A small sign in a window reads: "Coxsackie Correspondence Conservatory of Music." The only LIGHT comes from a blinking neon sign outside. LILY and HYDE enter joking and laughing. SHE tuns on the LIGHT.

LILY. Well, Eddie, this is it. My casa pequeño. You make yourself comfy. *I'll* get the bubbly.

(*SHE exits to the kitchen. HYDE snoops about the room, looks at her porno, sniffs her panties, licks her shoes, tries on her bra, etc. over the following.*)

HYDE. What's all this sheet music for?
LILY. (*Offstage.*) Oh, didn't I tell you? I have a degree from Yale in musicology.

HYDE. (*Picks up a dildo.*) Do you play an instrument?
LILY. I sing.
HYDE. Of course.
LILY. And I teach opera. I don't sing opera myself. Don't have the natural placement, although that's not really important. In short, I didn't have the talent. So I decided to devote my life to teaching. I am the sole director of the Coxsackie Correspondance Conservatory of Music.

(*SOUND of a champagne cork popping. HYDE is startled as the cork hits him in the head, and hides what HE's doing.*)

HYDE. And The Fruit Bowl?
LILY. (*Enters with two glasses of champagne.*) A girl's got to have an outlet. And besides, opera barely keeps me in lipstick, never mind the bills. I have to work day and night to keep the conservatory afloat.
HYDE. Your devotion is touching, Lily my dear.
LILY. Well, here's to misspent devotion.

(*Toasts her glass. He returns the toast. THEY both drink. When he is finished gulping his down, HE burps loudly.*)

LILY. Real attractive, Eddie.
HYDE. That's the second time you've said I'm attractive. I'm so glad you feel that way, Lily, because I find *you* irresistible!

(*HE grabs her. SHE pushes him away.*)

LILY. Well try resisting! Hey, what's gotten into you?
HYDE. It's what I want to put into *you*, Lily.

(*HE pulls out his tiny, dog-like penis. SHE screams.*)

LILY. Do I know how to pick 'em ... Again I get a raw deal!

HYDE. Your kind always does. (*He begins playing with himself as HE slowly approaches her.*) Come now, Lily. Come to Eddie. I'll cheat you and humiliate you, but I'll give you moments of utter blackness and refreshment and rebirth such as you've never had before.

LILY. (*Pulling away.*) I invited you up for a little fun and a bottle of burps, not a black mass. Just who do you think you are?

HYDE. A caged beast which delights in horror and destruction; the wickedest man in all Coxsackie; the only one who's good enough for you.

(*HE jumps on her back. SHE flips him off.*)

LILY. You really know how to build up a girl's ego.

(*SHE slaps his hands as HE feels her up.*)

HYDE. Oh ... these elementary sensations of pleasure are exquisite. Doctor Jekyll's reactions to...

(*SHE stops protesting.*)

HYDE. ... such carnal abundance would be like that of saintly Anchorites in their cells tempted by voluptuous visions.

LILY. (*Getting aroused.*) Oh, yeah. That's hot. Tell me all about Henry Jekyll.

HYDE. All right, Lily. First of all he wouldn't do that ... (*HE slaps her face.*) Or this ...

(*Laughing, HE strikes her again. SHE falls to the bed.*)

LILY. Ow!!! Stop it, ya big lug!!!

HYDE. Not till I've told you *all* about him. (*HE handcuffs her to the bedpost.*)

LILY. What are you doing? No, Eddie, please!!!

HYDE. Too late, my dear. You'll soon know what a sad man Henry Jekyll is ... frittering away mortality when he could have all this. Oh, what a lovely slave you'll make for Mr. Hyde.

LILY. I'm nobody's slave!

HYDE. Then call me nobody.

LILY. I'm not kidding anymore, Eddie! Let me go!

HYDE. Don't be silly, Lily. The fun's just beginning.

LILY. This isn't what I call fun, Eddie! Didn't anyone ever teach you that the body is the temple of the soul?

HYDE. Yes. Some people's bodies are temples, but *yours* is an amusement park, and I want to sample every bit of it from the roller coaster to the fun house with a few wet and wild water rides thrown in.

LILY. This is more like the house of horror! If you don't stop it, I'll tell Doctor Jekyll.

HYDE. Oooh, you will will you? And just what are you gonna tell him?

LILY. How could anyone like Henry Jekyll be associated with the likes of you? He's a brilliant man, and let's face it ... somebody blew out the candle in your pumpkin a long time ago.

HYDE. Tell the good doctor whatever you like, but watch what you say to me, Lily. You're makin' me as horny as a hop-toad.

LILY. Yeah? You kinda look like one too!

HYDE. That's right! Get angry!

LILY. Ah, go thud your pud somewhere else! God! I've had warts that went away quicker!

HYDE. (*Mauling her.*) Oh, yes! That's what I like. Scurvy, scabies, stabs and sores. Herpes, rabies, crabs from whores. I want it all!
LILY. (*Violently pushes him away.*) You sick pig!!!
HYDE. There are little few insults you could hurl upon me that wouldn't be true ... this I know. But my total wickedness gives me a total freedom you shall never know!!! Under your fast talk, paint, powder and press-on-nails ...

(*HE tears off one of her nails. SHE screams.*)

HYDE. ... lies a heart of pure gold ... You'll succumb to me, Lily!
LILY. Never!!!

(*HE punches her in the jaw, knocking her out cold. HE then begins to feel her up and remove her clothes.*)

HYDE. You'll see, my dear Magdalene. The goodness in you is strong, and like in the past you'll try to redeem this lost soul ...

(*HE tickles her foot which brings her around. SHE tries desperately but in vain to free herself as HE stands up on the bed, threatening her and slowly removes his jacket, revealing his hideous form.*)

HYDE. ... but his evil towers over your good and he'll drag you to hell with him. Neither your kindness nor loathing will reveal the angel from my soul. (*HE unzips his pants.*) You'll see only the monster from its pit! Mr. Hyde's gone wilding!!!

(*HE dives on Lily like a hungry carnivore. SHE screams. LIGHTS out.*)

ACT I

Scene 5

SCENE: The Jekyll home four weeks later. It is early afternoon. MINERVA is dusting things with a feather duster. MARY JEKYLL is seated in a chair reading the paper.

MINERVA. Mrs. J, the dust keeps comin' back no matter how much I try to get rid of it. Did it ever occur to you that dust is part of God's plan and we're wrong to remove it?
MARY. No.
MINERVA. Just a thought.
MARY. I'm worried about Henry coming home so late every night. It says here that a crime wave has struck Coxsackie.
MINERVA. (*Laughs.*) I'm sorry, Mrs. J. But a crime wave in Coxsackie could be five Jaywalkers and a flasher. This town's nothing more than a cemetery with lights.
MARY. Have you forgotten the Basil Hickock case, just a few short weeks ago?
MINERVA. How could I forget? That's where Doctor J spends most of his nights. Can't they just give Basil a night light or something?
MARY. If only it were that easy. Basil's been depressed ... I don't get it, Minerva. that man makes hamburger out of sixteen people, and what happens? Whatever Basil wants

Basil gets. Well, I'm depressed too, and I'm not asking for much. Just my husband one or two nights a week.

MINERVA. He sacked out on the couch again?

MARY. He might just as well spend *all* his nights on the couch. He's just as useful there as he is in bed.

MINERVA. (*Shocked.*) Mrs. J!!!

MARY. I'm sorry, Minerva. I didn't mean that ... entirely. But he barely notices me anymore. Maybe *I* should take up hatchet murdering as a hobby.

MINERVA. Opera's bad enough.

MARY. Well!

(*The DOORBELL rings.*)

MINERVA. That must be the mail. (*Exits.*)

MARY. Sometimes I wonder why we keep that woman on.

MINERVA. (*Offstage.*) Thanks again, Mr. Hoskins. (*Enters with the mail.*) Let's see ... bill, bill, junk mail, bill ... Oh, here, Mrs. J. This is for you. (*Hands Mary a package.*)

MARY. Oh, goody. It's my new opera lesson! (*SHE tears open the package and pulls out a cassette tape, libretto, letter, and Afro-wig.*) Wonderful! It's *Aida!* And there's a personal letter. (*Reads.*) "Dear Mary Jekyll: Congratulations! You have been chosen by the Coxsackie Correspondence Conservatory of Music to take part in our private tutelage program. (*To Minerva.*) Well, Minerva. What do you think of that? Only three weeks ago I received my first lesson and this says that next Thursday a Miss Lily Gay will come *here* to give me private instructions at *no* extra cost.

MINERVA. Lily Gay? Hmmm ... that name's familiar.

MARY. She happens to be the artistic director of the conservatory. We'll be working on scenes from *Lucia de*

Lammermoor by Donizetti. (*Pronounces it Lucy-ah die lame her maim her more by Donny Zeetee. Then SHE reads.*) Your audio-cassette tape and libretto will arrive this Friday by special delivery ... That's tomorrow. Oh, Minerva, this is thrilling!
MINERVA. Yeah.
MARY. I'll get right to work on *Aida*. I want to impress Miss Gay with my power of retention. Where's my Walkman?
MINERVA. It's in on your writing table.
MARY. Thank you, Minerva. Wish me luck.
MINERVA. Yeah, good luck ...

(*MARY exits. MINERVA continues to clean.*)

MINERVA. *Aida* ... Power of retention ... At least she'll have *something* to impress this Gay woman with.

(*MARY's screeching musical warm-ups are heard off.*)

MINERVA. Ooohhh, Lord in heaven above! She doesn't need luck, she needs a miracle. She's got a voice like prune juice. It goes right through you.

(*The DOORBELL rings.*)

MINERVA. I'll get it! (*SHE answers the door.*) Doctor Braintwain, come in.
BERNICE. (*Enters with MINERVA.*) Thank you, Minerva. Is Doctor Jekyll in?
MINERVA. He's *in* the laboratory. I'll get him for you.
BERNICE. Thanks.

(*As MINERVA goes to get Henry, HE enters.*)

BERNICE. Ah, here he is. Good afternoon, Henry.
HENRY. Bernice. I wasn't expecting you.
BERNICE. Well, I was expecting *you*, Henry, at the Institute three hours ago. There was a board meeting this morning.
HENRY. Strange ... I'd remember forgetting something *that* big.
BERNICE. What's the matter, Henry? You haven't been yourself lately.
HENRY. Perhaps *none* of us are what we appear to be, Bernice.
MINERVA. That's for sure.
HENRY. Excuse me, Minerva. Could you make us some coffee?
MINERVA. I thought you didn't like my coffee.
HENRY. I don't. But it's essential for my ... Oh, never mind.

(*MINERVA exits.*)

BERNICE. What did you say about Minerva's coffee being essential for something?
HENRY. For my ... my bowels. Got to keep things in good working order.
BERNICE. Maybe you should eat more roughage. But, speaking of working order, where have you been lately? I'm never able to find you at the Institute. You've been neglecting all your patients including Basil Hickock, and the meeting this morning was your chance to impress the board.
HENRY. I no longer need the support of the Institute for what you've called "balderdash." I've had a great deal of success with my "silly" experiments.

BERNICE. (*Dashed.*) I see ... so all the while you've been on salary at the Institute, you've been spending your time free-lancing. Who is it, Henry? Some big pharmaceutical company, or maybe the Pentagon?

HENRY. My funding is from a private source. An independently wealthy benefactor who must remain nameless.

BERNICE. Not the one who calls himself Edward Hyde, the wickedest man in all Coxsackie?

HENRY. What?!!!

BERNICE. So it's true. Why else would you have anything to do with the likes of that half-baked stand-up comedian?

HENRY. You know Mr. Hyde?

BERNICE. As well as anyone can know a monster. Henry, with your experience among the mentally deranged, even you must admit there's no other case like him.

HENRY. Yes. I'll admit that.

BERNICE. Then you know he's a total psychopath, without any regard for the laws of morality or the state, and without fear of the consequences of his wicked acts. He seeks only to satisfy his own greed, totally without conscience. He's evil, Henry! And whatever you're doing for him can only beget evil! I know a girl ... Lily. The girl I brought to you weeks ago who was involved with Basil Hickock. She's lived in fear of Hyde ever since she met him. He's trying to break her spirit and is destroying her body and mind along with it. Does he have the same control over you and your work, Henry?

HENRY. You don't understand.

BERNICE. I do understand that mankind has continually misused science! Ever since Prometheus brought down fires from heaven ... But you, Henry, more than anyone I've ever known, are a man of integrity. To compromise yourself like this will destroy you.

MINERVA. (*Enters with a coffee service.*) Here's your java fix, Dr. J. Do you want me to pour?

HENRY. No, Minerva. I can handle it myself. (*Suddenly in HYDE's voice.*) Cock-suckin' father-fuckin' bitch!!!

MINERVA. What?!!!

HENRY. It was nothing ... I ... I ... burned myself on the pot. That's all. (*Again in HYDE's voice.*) Your mother sucks cocks in hell!

BERNICE. Henry, let me tend that burn for you.

MINERVA. It must be awfully bad. I've never heard a foul word out of Doctor J's mouth in all the time I've worked for him.

HENRY. It's really not bad. I can handle it.

MARY. (*Enters wearing an Afro-wig with libretto and tape player headphones.*) Oh, there you are, Henry. Hello, Doctor Braintwain. I have a little treat for you. I'm going to sing an aria from Verdi's *Aida*.

HENRY. (*In HYDE's voice.*) You eat a *what*, bitch?!

(*EVERYONE looks uncomfortable. MARY notices this.*)

MARY. What was that, Henry? ... Oh ... Is this a bad time?

MINERVA. No. But I have a feeling it's about to be.

MARY. Nonsense, Minerva. Now, try to imagine a hall in the Palace of the Pharoahs of Memphis.

HENRY. (*In HYDE's voice.*) Try to imagine an asshole the size of the Sphinx!

MARY. What was that, Henry?

HENRY. (*Slaps himself.*) Nothing, Mary my love. (*Then aside.*) My God, I'm transforming!

MARY. The beautiful Ethiopian princess Aida, enslaved by the Egyptians, is caught up in her love for

Egyptian captain of the guards Radames. She shouts to him, "Ritorna vincitor!"

HENRY. (*Echoes as HYDE*.) Rape the stinkin' whore!

MARY. (*Mis-hearing*.) Yes, Henry, "Ritorna vincitor," or "return when you have won." In an agitated and pathetic prayer Aida beseeches the gods to forgive her insane words, to destroy their oppressors, and to restore her to her royal father Amonasro.

HENRY. (*Again as HYDE*.) You're an asshole.

MARY. That's correct, Henry. Amonasro. I will appear to sing the entire thirty bar passage a capella. That is, *I* will hear the music but you won't because you don't have headphones.

MINERVA. (*Aside*.) I sure wish *I* did.

MARY. (*Pushes the "play" button on her tape deck and begins to sing/scream*.)

RITORNA VINCITOR! ... E DAL MIO LABBRO
USCÌ L'EMPIA PAROLA!
VINCITOR DEL PADRE MIO,
DI LUI CHE IMPUGNA L'ARMI PER ME,
PER RIDONARMI UNA PATRIA, UNA REGIA,
E IL NOME ILLUSTRE
CHE QUI CELAR M' E FORZA!

HENRY. (*Again as HYDE*.) Forza *you*, Bitch!!! (*HE jumps up, grabs the coffee and exits running into the laboratory, laughing maniacally*.) Ha ha ha ha!! Shit, piss, cock and doody!!!

MINERVA. That burn must really be bothering him.

BERNICE. (*To herself*.) He appears to be suffering from the most severe case of Tourette's Syndrome I've ever seen.

MARY. Dear Henry was moved to the very core of his soul by that splendid passage. What a sensitive man I married.

(*MARY is in ecstasy, BERNICE is puzzled, and MINERVA shrugs as HYDE howls offstage. LIGHTS out.*)

ACT I

Scene 6

SCENE: The Fruit Bowl that evening. It is stand-up night. LILY and ACULINE are having a serious conversation at one of the tables.

LILY. I've simply got to get away from him. He terrifies me.

ACULINE. Sounds like the princess finally discovered the frog is really a frog.

LILY. I gave him four of the best weeks of my life. Oh, how could I have been so wrong about someone?

ACULINE. I'd say you had a lifetime of practice.

LILY. You're right, Aculine. I should have known he was evil when he laughed at "The Song of Bernadette."

ACULINE. The macho pig! But Honey, a relationship *is* a two-way street.

LILY. Yeah. And I was run over in both lanes. Oh! Why do I get so mad at myself for getting so mad at someone who makes me so mad?

ACULINE. Stop being so hard on yourself. That's *my* job. Lily child, you ought to be mad at him. Look at the marks he's left on you. I'd shoot the sucker dead if he did that to me. (*SHE pulls out a pistol.*)

LILY. I don't want to kill him, I just want him out of my life permanently ... Do you always carry that?

ACULINE. Ever since I opened this place. "One never knows, do one?"

LILY. Am I ever proof of that. Aculine, I've got to get rid of him!

ACULINE. If there's anything I can do, Honey, just let me know.

LILY. Thanks. I knew I could count on you.

BERNICE. (*Enters with a drink and joins them.*) That first act wasn't bad ... a few jokes in it too. Who's up next?

ACULINE. Oh, someone with the personality and demeanor of a dung beetle. One guess.

BERNICE. By your charitable description I would say it's that slime-ball Eddie Hyde.

ACULINE. Bingo!

BERNICE. Well, I've got a chilling little tale for you.

ACULINE. (*Patting Bernice's behind.*) I know, but I think it's cute anyway.

BERNICE. Funny, Honey ... I went by Henry Jekyll's home this afternoon. It turns out he's doing some experimental work for Hyde.

LILY. What?!

BERNICE. Precisely my reaction, Lily. It seems the little troll is quite wealthy by means of an unknown source.

ACULINE. That *is* a grim little fairy tale. (*Pats Bernice's butt again.*) No offense ... He's probably a white slaver.

LILY. He *is* ... in a way ... Well, I don't know what he does for money, but I know what he does for free.

(*LILY shows them the bruises on her arm as HYDE enters and sneaks up behind them.*)

HYDE. What? You girls playing a friendly little game of connect-the-liver spots?

ACULINE. Cram it, clown!

HYDE. Just a little joke.

ACULINE. No, Eddie. A joke is when you make people laugh. Speakin' of ... are you ready to go on?

HYDE. (*Unzips his pants.*) Go on what?

LILY. Oh, gross!

HYDE. Hee hee hee ... Oh, I forgot. Have you heard? Lily's pee-shy.

LILY. (*Embarrassed, SHE runs up to him.*) I told you that in the strictest of confidence.

HYDE. Don't you ever learn? Lily, after your act tonight would you like to go out for a late supper?

LILY. Out with you? Over my dead body!

HYDE. Let's not bring up last night again.

LILY. I'd rather remove my own gall bladder with an oyster fork.

HYDE. Sounds appetizing, but I was thinking Chinese.

BERNICE. Why don't you leave her alone, Eddie?

HYDE. Ah, the other half of my favorite couple. Steve and Edie ... Amin.

BERNICE. Aren't you confusing this place with another where everyone isn't totally repulsed by your presence?

HYDE. Touché, Bernie.

ACULINE. That's enough! (*To Hyde getting up.*) I'm gonna announce you now, so be ready.

HYDE. We'll discuss this further. (*HE glares at Lily and Bernice threateningly.*)

ACULINE. (*At the microphone.*) Hello again, gang! Well, I now have the unpleasant job of introducing the next act. This guy thinks he's Don Juan, but he's more like "Dawn of the Dead." Some people think he's got a chip on his shoulder, but it's actually his head ... He is sooo ugly ...

BERNICE. How ugly is he?!!!

ACULINE. They used to push his face in the dough to make animal cookies ... If you don't get the picture by now, you're under anesthesia, or you oughta be ... without further ado ... about nothin' ... the man whose name will soon be a household pet ... The wickedest man in all Coxsackie ... Eddie Hyde! (*To Hyde.*) The floor is yours, and not for the first time I might add. (*SHE returns to Bernice and Lily.*)

HYDE. (*Takes the stage.*) Greetings and salivations! Thank you, Miss Aculine. How would we manage without her wit? Tell me, Aculine, how do *you* manage without it? ... For those of you who haven't caught my act before, I am Eddie Hyde, the wickedest man in all Coxsackie. Everyone says, if you can't say something nice, say it about Eddie. Well, whatever they say, it's probably true ... But that's enough about me. Have you met my girlfriend Lily? Maybe you've heard her sing here at The Fruit Bowl? She's got a great voice. It grates on everyone ... Come on, Lily! Take a bow.

(*LILY is humiliated but bows anyhow. APPLAUSE.*)

HYDE. Watch out, Hon. She's a little top-heavy ... Pretty, huh? How much of it do you think is real? I'm not just talkin' about the stuff you can take *off*, like false nails and lashes, color contact lenses, a pound of make-up, the wig, the jewelry, and clothes, what there are of them ... I'm talkin' about the stuff that's *on* permanently ... Nice teeth, huh? It's actually one tooth that wraps all the way around ... Check out the cheek bones, hips, and those massive headlights. This girl has enough silicone in her to be legally declared a "Mattel" doll ... Put a wick in her and she'd burn for a month ... And you think that's a cute dimple? Another face lift and she'll have a beard ... But looks aren't everything. There's something magic about her, and more people have enjoyed that magic than Harry Houdini's ... She's also very artistic. In fact, she's seen more ceilings than Michelangelo ... Yes, she's a real culture vulture ... I told you she's musical, right? Well, for her birthday I got her a dozen roses and a piano, but she told me she'd rather have two lips on an organ ... economical, huh? ... And smart too. Her brain is so big, sometimes I can actually hear it grind to a halt ... It's only the little things she has problems with. Like she doesn't know the difference between a blow-job and a "Big Mac" which makes her a real ball at lunch time ... But she does know that soy beans and dildos are both meat-substitutes ... Boy can she make a mean dildo-loaf ... Not that a dildo gets to loaf much around her place ... I went to her place the other night. When I opened the door a bald rooster comes running out. I walk in and find her spitting out feathers. She told me she was sucking a cock ...Which reminds me, I bought her a dildo for company when Eddie's not around, sorta to make ends meet ... Well, she told me she didn't like it, I asked why, she said it chipped her teeth ... I wonder what she thinks a "water-pic" is for? ... Well, I guess that's enough about Lily for now. Did you hear the one about the queer burglar? He couldn't blow the safe so he went down on the elevator ... (*Boos from the audience.*) What do you call two gay guys named Bob? Oral Roberts ... (*More boos.*) What do you call this? (*Sticks out his tongue.*) A lesbian with a hard-on. (*More boos.*)

ACULINE. (*Outraged, SHE gets up.*) That does it! That ugly homophobic pig's outta here!

HYDE. Well, it looks like my time's up. Give me a big hand. (*EVERYONE claps .*) You call *that* a big hand? I couldn't get a hard-on all night with a hand like that ...

You've been a great audience. Like dead people without the rouge ... (*More boos.*) How long is the wimp convention in town?!

ACULINE. (*Approaching the stage.*) Hold on, low life!!!

HYDE. Ah, Aculine the boss-lady. The woman that thinks Chardonnay is a lovely name for a child.

ACULINE. What did you say, sucker?

HYDE. Sucker? Surely you're confusing me with Lily. That's *her* forte.

ACULINE. You've upset the crowd, you've upset Lily, but worst of all you got *me* upset! I want you out of my club, turkey! Right now!

HYDE. Gobble-gobble ... Very well, we're leaving. Come along, Lily. (*HE grabs Lily's arm and pulls her up.*)

LILY. No, Eddie. I don't want to go.

HYDE. (*Squeezing her arm till she kneels in pain.*) None of us want to go, my dear. But we've all got to go sometime.

BERNICE. (*Pulls Lily to her.*) Forget it, Hyde! She's staying right here. As for you ... can I escort you to the gutter?

HYDE. As soon as I'm joined by my lovely girl friend. (*Pulls Lily back to him.*) Now, Lily, are you coming?

LILY. No, Eddie! I'm leaving you for good.

HYDE. Well, I could understand if you left me for *bad*, but to leave me for *good?*

(*LILY pulls away from him.*)

ACULINE. Ya know, the lord ruined a good asshole when he put teeth in you mouth.

BERNICE. Get out, Hyde!

HYDE. (*Grabbing at Lily.*) Come here, you debauched doxy!!!!

ACULINE. (*Pulls out her pistol.*) Jump back, Jack! You take another step towards her and I'm gonna blow your brass balls off! Now get your ugly ass outta here right now!!!

HYDE. Since you put it that way, I'll leave. I don't want to overstay my welcome ... Think of me, Lily.

LILY. As if I had any choice!!! You're *all* I think about.

HYDE. Yes. And you always will. After awhile you won't know dreams from reality. I can already see the effects the toxins of fatigue are having on you. But I, on the other hand, don't tire. My evil, kept awake by ambition, is alert and swift to seize the occasion. I'll follow you everywhere ... like a nightmare presence biding its time I'll leap out on you when you least expect it, then pass away like a stain of breath upon a mirror... (*Exiting, HE glares threateningly at Lily.*) What's around the corner, Lily?

(*HE exits. Everyone is relieved. Suddenly HYDE bursts back into the room. LILY screams.*)

HYDE. What's behind that door?! Ha ha ha ha ha ...

BERNICE. You degenerate! You're filth! Don't listen to this vermin, Lily!

HYDE. With nightmare intensity all your thoughts will be held by the grappling hooks of Mr. Hyde's words and gestures. Nothing can protect you now!

ACULINE. (*Points her gun at him.*) Except me! Get out, sucker!

HYDE. (*To Lily.*) I'll fix you, my pretty!!! Ha ha ha ha ha ...

(*HYDE gives Lily a kick as HE exits laughing. SHE turns to Bernice and falls into her arms weeping uncontrollably. LIGHTS out.*)

ACT I

Scene 7

SCENE: A dimly lit street corner minutes later. HYDE walks along mumbling to himself. A JEHOVAH'S WITNESS stands on a corner with a sandwich-board on. It read something like: A new advent of Jehovah is upon us! Repent! Faith heals all! Etc.!

HYDE. I'll kill the bitch! That's what I'll do. She can't do this to Edward Hyde and get away with it. I'll cancel her subscription to life! Ha ha ha ha ha!!!

J.W. "A sower went out to sow his seed: and as he sowed, some fell by the wayside; and it was trodden down, and the fowls of the air devoured it. And some fell upon a rock; and as soon as it was sprung up, it withered away, because it lacked moisture. And some fell among thorns; and the thorns sprang up with it; and choked it. And others fell on good ground, and sprang up, and bare fruit a hundred-fold!"

HYDE. What's this? A little late for a Future Farmers of America meeting isn't it?

J.W. Come to Jehovah, friend. He'll turn your life around.

HYDE. Yeah? That's what Jim Jones said before he spiked the punch.

J.W. I can help you, son.

HYDE. I can help myself, dad!

J.W. The important thing in this life is to find the inner peace which brings true happiness.

HYDE. Where's you get that? On a "Hallmark" card? What do you want anyhow?

J.W. I'm searching out sinners for Jehovah.

HYDE. Well, when you find some, save a couple for me too.

J.W. But, brother! Don't you have any faith?

HYDE. I have knowledge, *good* man! And knowledge is the enemy of faith!

J.W. But there are great masses of the earth's people who put their faith in the Lord.

HYDE. I don't approve of the masses. It's a passion-governed world and I go with the flow ... I have a certain *sin*-sibility to uphold.

J.W. But the wages of sin is death and eternal damnation in the pit of hell!

HYDE. Heaven or hell ... I'll bet whatever we're going to looks a lot like where we're coming from

J.W. Well, I hope the Lord Jehovah has mercy on your soul; he certainly didn't have any on your face.

HYDE. Well, we all have our burdens.

J.W. "Take my yoke upon you, and learn of me; for I am meek and lowly in heart: and ye shall find rest unto your souls. For my yoke is easy, and my burden light."

HYDE. How light? (*HE pulls off the J.W.'s sandwich board and begins to beat him with it.*) It *is* light!

J.W. Get thee behind me, Satan!

HYDE. Okay. (*HE walks behind the J.W. and continues beating him.*)

J.W. Help! Help!

HYDE. Oh, you must be calling on your god to help you, 'cause there's certainly no one else around.

J.W. What manner of man is this?

HYDE. (*Still beating him.*) You're the devil's playground and I don't want to let my hands go idle on me!

J.W. Oh, my God!

HYDE. No. You can call me Eddie Hyde. The wickedest man in all Coxsackie. Prepare to meet thy maker!

J.W. Forgive him, Lord! Remember he's your fault!

(*HYDE laughs as HE beats the man to death. Police SIRENS are heard approaching. HYDE runs out, accidentally dropping his wallet at the scene. LIGHTS out.*)

End of Act I

ACT II

Scene 1

SCENE: HENRY JEKYLL's laboratory one week later. It is Thursday morning. HENRY paces back and forth speaking his thoughts aloud and recording them on his tape deck.

HENRY. I feel like an accident victim crawling from the wreckage. Is Dr. Jekyll responsible for what Mr. Hyde does? ... Yes. For it was I who split the soul in two. It was I who dared to challenge God for this supreme ejaculation of egotism, and it is I who must do my best to atone for these unholy deeds ... My God ... Murder ... And Lily ... The mess I've made of the poor kid's life. Hyde seduced her with his knowledge of me ... Doctor Jekyll, a man to be admired and trusted ... But aren't these base tendencies within every man? Doesn't every man have a hidden desire to create that one, perfect magnum opus? That flawless, unsolvable Créme de la Crime? It's almost evolution's law ... I am in no way trying to justify or absolve my wicked brother Hyde from the crimes he ... *we* have committed. But I swear that I will continue, as I have since the murder a week ago this very day, to make amends for our damnable sins. (*HE takes a vial of the formula from his pocket.*) I would destroy the formula too, if I didn't need it to prevent Mr. Hyde from returning ... As I've gotten weaker, he's become so much stronger. It demands every ounce of force my mind and body can muster to constrain him. Must I become Hyde in spite of my better self? Every fiber of my body now craves the potion. He's tasted blood and liked it. How much longer can I hold him off?

(*There is a KNOCK at the door. HE turns off the tape deck.*)

HENRY. Yes? What is it?
MINERVA. (*Offstage.*) It's Minerva, Doctor J. Doctor Braintwain's here.
HENRY. (*Sotto voce.*) Shit!!! (*Gets the door.*) Thank you, Minerva. Hello, Bernice.
BERNICE. (*Entering.*) Hello, Henry. I was just driving by and thought I'd stop in to see how you're doing.
HENRY. I'm quite well, thank you. Just finished taping some notes.
BERNICE. Notes?
HENRY. Observations on a patient of mine.
BERNICE. I'd like to talk to you about something.
HENRY. (*In earnest.*) Is there a problem? If there's anything at all I can do ...
BERNICE. No, no, no, it's nothing like that. What it is ... well, I never thought I'd hear myself say this, but I think you're over-doing it, Henry.
HENRY. What do you mean?
BERNICE. Ever since the murder last week you've been working double time at full-speed, and it's showing. Not in your work ... You're the best! But you look so tired. Ease up on yourself. You're not responsible for what Hyde did. The police know he tried to frame you for the murder when he left your wallet at the scene of the crime. It's a lucky thing that housewife saw the whole thing from her window ... not lucky for *her* of course. She's now under my care. To think, it could have been Lily he'd beaten to death that night if Aculine hadn't sent him on his way.
HENRY. How is Lily?

BERNICE. Much better, but still a little shaken. She's been under police protection since the murder.

HENRY. So have we.

BERNICE. I know. I saw the patrolman outside. You and Lily were Hyde's only friends, which oddly enough puts you in the most danger. A familiar paradox ... You know, I'm beginning to think we have another Basil Hickock on our hands. Perhaps, like Basil, there's another Edward Hyde out there somewhere who's able to function normally.

HENRY. You're beginning to sound a little like Henry Jekyll, Bernice.

BERNICE. (*Worried.*) How?

HENRY. I thought you'd ruled out the possibility of Quantum Synaptic Dualism.

BERNICE. I'm not ruling anything out anymore, Henry.

HENRY. I'm sorry for the trouble Hyde has caused.

BERNICE. Well, it's certainly not your fault. But there's something puzzling me. Why did you tell the police that Hyde is a patient of yours?

HENRY. Because I couldn't reveal my experiment to them. They'd never understand. If he's a patient, my involvement is minimal, but if he's my benefactor ... that's another story. I'd appreciate it if you didn't say anything.

BERNICE. No problem. But what if Hyde returns?

HENRY. Mark my words ... he'll never be heard of again.

(*From this point on it's as though HYDE is trying to take over Henry's body. BERNICE doesn't notice.*)

BERNICE. Well, I hope you're right. If it came to trial, you'd definitely be involved. I can't say that I care what becomes of Mr. Hyde, but I couldn't stand to see your good name sucked down in this eddy of scandal. The police chief is even talking about getting the case on America's Most Wanton.

HENRY. What's that?

BERNICE. One of those new, at-home vigilante programs on television. People call in with information about criminals who are on the lam. It brings out the "Big Brother" in everyone.

HENRY. Just the same, I'm quite confident we've seen the last of the beast.

BERNICE. Good. Well, Henry, I've got to be going. You could take a couple days off, if you like. I'd be happy to see to your patients for you. Remember, all work and no play makes Jekyll a dull boy.

HENRY. Pretty corny, Bernice. Thanks for the offer.

BERNICE. Please, try taking it easy, if not for your sake, for mine. The last thing I need is for my best doctor and most celebrated scientist to stress-out on me.

HENRY. I appreciate your concern. I'll see you later. (*HE rushes her towards the door.*)

BERNICE. All right, Henry. But if you change your mind ...

HENRY. You'll be the first to know.

BERNICE. Good. Goodbye, Henry.

HENRY. Bye, Bernice. Thanks again.

(*SHE exits. HE closes the door and calms himself.*)

HENRY. Ah, Bernice my dear friend. If only I could be honest with you. Emerson said, "A friend is a person with whom I may be sincere. Before him, I may think aloud." Do I have a friend who would not recoil with horror upon discovering my secret? When I befriended Hyde, I renounced all other friendships ... and now I am as alone as he is ...

His secret is safe with me, but can I rely upon him to keep mine? Therefore, he must never come again! (*HE begins to change again.*) You devil! Your will to survive is strong! "Stand still you moving spheres of heaven, that time may cease, and 'Mr. Hyde' never come!" (*HE changes fully into MR. HYDE.*)

HYDE. I must keep you in your place, good Doctor Henry Jekyll. I'll take no more orders from you, friend and brother.

(*A KNOCK at the door.*)

HYDE. Who is that?
MARY. (*Offstage.*) Henry? Is that you?
HENRY. What do you want?
MARY. My guests will be arriving shortly and you promised to sit in on my opera lesson.
HYDE. She's gotta be kidding. I heard her sing the other day. I thought someone was killing chickens out back.
MARY. I want you to get your mind off this Mr. Hyde and share this moment of glory with me.
HYDE. It's a moment of glory all right. Blink and you'll miss it.
MARY. What was that, dear?
HYDE. Nothing, Mary, my love. I'll be out shortly.
MARY. All right, Henry, but hurry.
HYDE. Well, Doctor. Perhaps I'd be wise to conceal myself within you a little longer. (*HE pulls out the vial and looks about.*) Coffee! The cursed catalyst! There's none here. I hope the serving wench has prepared some of the hideous brew ... (*LIGHTS out as HE exits.*)

ACT II

Scene 2

SCENE: The Jekyll living room seconds later. HYDE enters but hides when HE hears someone coming. MINERVA enters carrying a tray with coffee service. MARY follows her with sandwiches and cakes. THEY set these down. MARY wears a full-length kilt.

MARY. Do you think there'll be enough sandwiches, Minerva?

MINERVA. Don't worry about it. I can always make some more.

MARY. Oh, I'm so nervous.

MINERVA. Gee, I never noticed ... Mrs. J, I didn't think you were the trendy type.

MARY. What on earth do you mean?

MINERVA. Did you know that dress is on backwards?

MARY. What?! Oh my God! She'll be here any minute! Help me, Minerva!

MINERVA. All right, Mrs. J! Just calm down!

MARY. (*Exiting in a dither.*) Oh, dear. Lily Gay!

MINERVA. Oh, for cryin' out cats and dogs, Mrs. J!

(THEY exit in a hurry. HYDE enters and goes to the coffee tray, pours the contents of the vial into the coffee pot, pours himself a cup and toasts.)

HYDE. From rosy dreams to gray reality! (*HE drinks and begins to convulse.*) I'll be waiting in our little limbo, Henry my brother with the saintly conscience. Brother? We're more like Siamese-strangers. Ah! (*HE is wracked with pain.*) And remember, if you try to entomb me again, my retaliation will ruin you.

(*The DOORBELL rings wildly.*)

HYDE. Oh, it's the doorbell. I thought it was the "Good Humor" man.

(*The DOORBELL rings again.*)

MINERVA. (*Offstage.*) Coming!!! Coming!!!

(*HYDE exits. MINERVA enters furious as the BELL continues to ring.*)

MINERVA. Hold your horses! I'm coming! (*SHE gets the door.*) Oh, it's you, what's-your-name!
LILY. (*Offstage.*) Lily Gay.
MINERVA. Yeah. That's it.
LILY. Well, I usually get it right ... You're Minerva?
MINERVA. That's right. Now what do you want?
LILY. (*Pushes her way into the room followed by ACULINE, who is dressed as a man.*) I have an appointment with Mrs. Jekyll.
MINERVA. Are your sure you're not here to throw yourself at *Doctor* Jekyll again?
LILY. What's with you?
MINERVA. Mrs. J said you're a woman of taste and intelligence. I've seen no evidence of that.
LILY. I sure wish I could bottle that charm of yours.
MINERVA. Yeah?
LILY. Then I could put a cork in it.
ACULINE. (*Stops the impending cat-fight. In a bad Italian accent.*) Thata face! Que faccia bella!
MINERVA. (*Immediately charmed.*) Oh ... I haven't had the pleasure.

LILY. I'm not surprised! ... He's the famous Italian basso Signore Luigi Aculini.

ACULINE. You like-a opera?

MINERVA. Not really. But *you're* kinda cute.

ACULINE. I'ma glada youa thinka so, Minerva. Ah, Minerva ... It'sa like-a musica. Maybe soma time we canna getta togetha?

MINERVA. Maybe so, Signore ...

ACULINE. (*Kissing her hand.*) Luigi Aculini.

MINERVA. Luigi ... I'll see if Mrs. J's ready yet. And go easy on her, huh? The woman's porch light has been flickering for years.

ACULINE. Of coursa. (*THEY flirt as MINERVA exits.*) How was that for fancy footwork?

LILY. Great! Now she thinks you're in love with her Italiano style.

ACULINE. Well, I wouldn't kick her out of *my* bed for eating crackers.

LILY. Why else would she be there?

ACULINE. I hope that's not in reference to my preference? ... Boy, she's harder to get through than those cops out front.

(*HENRY enters unnoticed and stands next to Lily.*)

LILY. I'll say. This is the first time I've ever felt good about being escorted around by a cop. (*SHE sees Henry and screams. Startled HE jumps up and SHE catches him in her arms.*) Oooooohhhh!!! Doctor Jekyll.

HENRY. Are you all right, Lily?

LILY. (*Putting him down.*) For the moment, Doctor. But I don't know how much longer. I've been feeling like a perfect candidate for the laughing academy ever since Eddie Hyde threatened to kill me.

HYDE. Try to relax, Lily. Come sit down. (*SHE sits.*)

ACULINE. Doctor Jekyll, my name's Aculine. I'm Lily's friend.

HENRY. (*Shakes her hand.*) It's a pleasure to finally meet you, Aculine. Bernice has told me all about you.

ACULINE. Not *all* I hope.

HENRY. Why the costume?

ACULINE. I'm a last minute basso.

HENRY. Really?

ACULINE. Actually, Lily needed some, pardon-the-expression, moral support. You see, the only reason she planned all this opera lesson business with your wife was to ...

LILY. Doctor, you've just got to help me! It's just like Eddie Hyde said, "Like a nightmare presence biding its time ..." He hasn't been around for a week but I expect him to pop up out of the toilet or something any minute like "Freddy Kruger." I'm even afraid to sleep because he usually shows up in my dreams to hack me to pieces.

HENRY. Like Basil Hickock or Louie the Lunger. Hmmm ... You do have a history of relationship with this sort of fellow.

LILY. Can I help it? I'm like a magnet to guys like that.

HENRY. Before you relive a mistake you should remember the past results.

ACULINE. It's a little late for all this. She needs help now.

HENRY. You're right ... Maybe he just said all that to try winning you back. Perhaps his threats were merely the last act of a desperate man?

ACULINE. We don't care if it's the first act of "Cat on a Hot Tin Roof!" That psycho threatened her life, and he's killed once already! Bernie says you're the only one who has any kind of control over Hyde.

HENRY. Yes. Of course. I'm sorry. I don't know what I can do, but I promise to stop the wretch if he shows up again. (*HE is suddenly seized with pain.*) Agh! But you must excuse me for the moment.

(*HENRY runs out of the room. ACULINE and LILY look at each other confused. MARY and MINERVA enter. MARY is a sight in her Scottish outfit complete with bagpipes. LILY stands.*)

MARY. I hope I didn't keep you waiting too long.
LILY. Not at all.
MARY. Miss Lily Gay, I presume? (*Shakes Lily's hand.*) I'm Mrs. Jekyll but please call me Mary.
LILY. It's a pleasure to meet you, Mary. I would like to introduce Signore Luigi Aculini.
MINERVA. (*Making sweet-eyes at Aculine.*) He's a famous Italian basso.
MARY. Well, I'm certainly honored, Signore Aculini.
ACULINE. The honor's alla mine-a. (*Kisses her hand.*)
MARY. Oh, so charming. Minerva, where is Henry? I told him not ten minutes ago to come join us.
LILY. He was here a moment ago but left suddenly.
MINERVA. (*Glaring at Lily.*) I'll bet!
MARY. Henry's become so unpredictable. Lately, when he's here, it's rather like having a live volcano in the house.
MINERVA. Yes. And we're trying to avoid eruptions.
ACULINE. Canna we begina without him?
MARY. Yes, of course, Signore Luigi. I'm so eager to start. In fact, I've already done my vocal warm-ups.
MINERVA. And they were the best vocal warm-ups I've ever heard.
MARY. Why, thank you, Minerva. That's quite a compliment.

MINERVA. Not if you heard the others.

LILY. Mary ... Before we begin, I'd like to say that I think you're a very brave woman taking up opera at your age. Not that you're old, but most singers begin as girls. Any other woman wouldn't even bother to try.

MARY. Neither would the old Mary Jekyll. But the *new* Mary Jekyll's willing to take chances. Go out on a limb. I don't care if I look like a total fool to the rest of the world.

MINERVA. Sounds like the *old* Mary Jekyll to me.

LILY. (*Aside to Mary.*) How do you stand her?

MARY. (*Sincere.*) I don't have to. She stands all by herself.

MINERVA. Is there something you'd like to say to me, Ms. Gay?

LILY. No, Minerva. I'm trying to keep from telling you something.

MARY. Minerva, are you being rude to my guest?

MINERVA. (*Aside to Mary.*) Mrs. J, I know that tamale. She spends more time on her back than a garage mechanic.

MARY. The poor dear. I didn't know she was ill.

(*HENRY enters.*)

MARY. Oh, Henry. Come. Come sit down.

HENRY. Did I miss anything, Mary my dear?

MARY. Not a thing. We're just about to begin.

MINERVA. (*Spots LILY helping Henry to his seat.*) And I'm just about to finish ...

ACULINE. (*Coming to the rescue.*) Minerva my dearesta, maybe there'sa parta inna this opera forra you too?

MINERVA. Oh, Signore Luigi. Me?

LILY. You don't have to, Minerva. I really don't want to put you out.

MINERVA. I wish I could say the same about you ... It's a mighty tempting offer, Signore Luigi.

ACULINE. I gotta lotsa more tempting offersa too.

LILY. Oh, very well, If Mrs. Jekyll ...

MARY. Please. Mary.

LILY. If Mary doesn't mind. Do you mind, Mary?

MINERVA. (*Aside.*) Does it appear she even has a mind?

MARY. Not at all. This is wonderful. Well, Henry. Didn't I tell you we'd have fun?

HENRY. Yes, my dear. But I'll forgive you.

LILY. We shall work on Act Three, Scene One of Gaetano Donizetti's *Lucia di Lammermoor*. Lucia's delirio. Mary, you will play Lucia, of course. Signore Aculini will sing Raimondo; I will sing the part of Normanno; and Minvera will sing the chorus.

MINERVA. I always liked that name ... Chorus.

LILY. (*Picks up her large audio cassette deck and straps it around her neck.*) Now, I will also conduct ... Does everyone read music?

MINERVA. Is a pig's pussy pork?

LILY. *That's* where I've seen you before!

ACULINE. (*Breaking them up.*) Coma now, ladies!

HENRY. Is this an opera lesson or an episode of "The Glamorous Ladies of Wrestling?"

MARY. I guess those stories about competition between divas in the opera world are all true.

LILY. (*Aside to Aculine.*) I'm gonna hit her so hard she'll wear out from bouncing.

ACULINE. That's great. Then I'm sure Doctor Jekyll'd be real thrilled about helpin' you out. Get a grip, girl friend.

MARY. Henry, if we happen to be swept away by the drama of the scene, I hope you don't mind if I let his lips touch mine.

HENRY. Touch your what?

LILY. There will be none of that since Normanno is simply the captain of the guard and Raimondo is Lucia's elderly tutor.

HENRY. You don't know my wife Mary.

LILY. Of course you know the story?

MARY. Why, yes ... of course.

MINERVA. Mrs. J, I thought you said you didn't have time to read the rest of the libretto?

MARY. (*Aside.*) Minerva!

LILY. As a warm-up we'll sing the first chorus together. This is a happy wedding celebration at Lammermoor Castle just before everyone hears from Raimondo that Lucia has stabbed her groom Arturo to death ... Now, I will give everyone his or her note. (*SHE does this with a pitchpipe going down the line. EACH sings the note.*) Lucia ... Raimondo ... Chorus ... and Normanno ... Now together.

(*HENRY is nearly blown off his seat by the sound. LILY looks worried.*)

MARY. It sounds like we're in tune.
MINERVA. Sounds like you're in pain.
LILY. Here we go ...

(*SHE pushes the play button as EVERYONE adjusts their music. LILY conducts as THEY all sing. It is cacophony. HENRY tries to be polite but can't help wincing.*)

LILY, ACULINE, & MINERVA. (*Singing.*)
D'IMMENSO GIUBILO
S'INNALZI UN GRIDO.
CORRA LA SCOCIA

DI LIDO IN LIDO;
E AVVERTA I PERFIDI
NOSTRI NEMICI
CHE A NOI SORRIDONO
LE STELLE ANCOR.

MARY. How did that sound, Henry?

HENRY. I'm speechless.

MARY. And that was just a warm-up. Wait till we get to the tragic part.

HENRY. That wasn't?

LILY. (*Aside.*) Maybe this wasn't such a good idea.

MINERVA. Well, how was I?

LILY. On a scale of one to ten, you haven't even stepped on the scale yet.

MARY. How was I, Miss Gay?

LILY. Well, Mary ... you ... you show some promise ...

MARY. Did you hear that, Henry? Promise!

MINERVA. Yeah. Promise you'll never sing again.

LILY. Minerva, would you go see if anyone else's wounds need salting.

ACULINE. (*Breaking them up yet again.*) Come, Minerva. I'ma gonna giva you soma private coaching.

MINERVA. No, thanks, Luigi. I'm just not in the singing mood.

ACULINE. Wella, that'sa the way the egga rollsa.

MARY. I think you're being a very poor sport, Minerva.

MINERVA. (*Very upset.*) Hey, aren't I allowed to have a bad day?!

HENRY. Sure. You give us plenty of them. Keep one for yourself.

MINERVA. Thanks a lot, Doctor J.

HENRY. It's nothing, Minerva.

DR. JEKYLL & MR. HYDE

MARY. Shall we continue? I can't wait for Henry to hear my aria.

HENRY. (*Aside.*) I'd rather clip my nails in a "Cusinart."

MARY. What was that, Henry dear?

HENRY. Perhaps we should have some refreshments before you continue?

MARY. Oh, Henry. Always a gentleman and the perfect host ... Very well, I'll pour. (*Pours coffee for everyone over the following.*) There's plenty of sandwiches and cakes. Please help yourselves.

MINERVA. Don't pour any coffee for me, Mrs. J. I don't mind making the stuff, but it's one thing that will never touch these lips.

LILY. As if there anything that wants to.

MINERVA. I've got some errands to run ... but I'll stay here if you really need me.

MARY. I think we'll be fine, Minerva. You may leave.

MINERVA. Thanks, Mrs. J. So long, Luigi. It's been real swell getting to know you.

ACULINE. (*Having drank some of the coffee/potion, SHE is twitching.*) The swelling'sa alla mine.

MINERVA. You know where to find me if you still want to hook up.

ACULINE. And when I finda you, I'ma gonna hooka you.

MINERVA. See you all later. (*Then to Lily.*) Except you.

LILY. (*Also crazed from the formula.*) Thank God!

(*MINERVA exits.*)

HENRY. Don't mind Minerva, Lily.

LILY. (*Wildly.*) She must have eaten something that didn't agree with her.

HENRY. It wouldn't dare.

(*THEY all drink more coffee together and begin retching and convulsing over the following.*)

HENRY. My God! I forgot Hyde put the formula into the coffee! Agh! They musn't see me transform! But what of them? ... They've only taken a small amount ... perhaps when it wears off, they won't know what hit them. I'll remove the rest. (*HE picks up the coffee pot and exits to his lab.*)

LILY. (*Monster-like.*) All right, mother-fuckers! Let's do this shitty scene! You! Bitch!

MARY. What is it, you mattress-backed cocksucker? (*SHE is shocked by the words coming from her own mouth.*)

LILY. Haul your stupid snatch over here and sing!

MARY. (*Getting into it.*) You got it, tuna-breath!

LILY. And, you! Devil-dyke!

ACULINE. You talkin' to me, you white-assed sack of shit?

LILY. That's right, tacky tits! Tune up that tuba and try it on next to dizz-ball over here.

MARY. Yeah! I want a real man to play with. Get your tube-steak over here, big boy. I'm ready and rarin' for ya!

ACULINE. There's not a pussy on earth that's ready for what I got.

MARY. Show me your dip-stick, smut-bucket!

LILY. Clam up!!! Remember, this is a fuckin' *mad* scene! The dizzy broad Lucia's hearin' things!

MARY. Yeah. I'm hearin' your mouth, asshole! Let's get on with it!

ACULINE. Fuck yes!

LILY. All right! Hit it!!! (*LILY hits the tape deck hard with her fist. The MUSIC begins, playing twice its normal*

speed. They scene turns into utter chaos as THEY sing wildly and gesture lewdly.)
   CHORUS. (Lucia, Raimondo & Normanno.)
"OH, DIRE MISFORTUNE,
OH, DAY OF SORROW,
WHAT GLOOMY ENDING OF HAPPY MORROW!
NIGHT CAST THY SHADOW O'ER OUR LAMENTING,
SOON FREE HER SPIRIT FROM BONDS OF EARTH.

OH, HEAV'N IN MERCY THE CRIME FORGIVE HER,
SAD WAS HER FATE, CRUEL HATRED'S PREY.

(MARY hits a real clinker. ACULINE and LILY push her away. SHE exits.)

RAIMONDO & NORMANNO.
"ECCOLA!
OH, SIGHT OF SORROW
AS FROM THE GRAVE ARISEN!

(During a very brief musical interlude LILY and ACULINE do a sort of Scottish sword dance. MINERVA enters with her hat and coat on and sees this.)

   MINERVA. Looks like the inmates are running the asylum. I'd better go while the gettin's good...

(SHE exits as MARY re-enters clutching a bloodied knife.)

   LUCIA:
I HEAR THE BREATHING OF HIS VOICE LOW AND TENDER,
THAT VOICE RESOUNDETH WITHIN MY HEART FOREVER!

EGARDO, WHY WERE WE PARTED?
EGARDO, SAY, WHY DIDST THOU LEAVE ME?
LET ME NOT MOURN THEE;
SEE, FOR THY SAKE I'VE ALL FORSAKEN,
I'VE ALL FORSAKEN.

WHAT SHUDDER DO I FEEL THROUGH MY VEINS?
MY HEART IS TREMBLING,
MY SENSES FAIL!

(*MARY stiffens up like a cartoon corpse and falls back ACULINE and LILY catch her. LIGHTS out.*)

ACT II

Scene 3

SCENE: Lily's flat, later that day. ACULINE has an ice pack on her head.

ACULINE. I'll say one thing for that Minerva. She sure can make a mean cup of joe.
LILY. (*Enters with her panty hose around her knees.*) That's for sure. I've never in my life had a caffeine rush like that.
ACULINE. Or a hangover afterwards. I'll have to get her recipe. Did you call Bernie?
LILY. Yeah. She's comin' over in a few minutes to pick ya up.
ACULINE. Thanks, honey.
LILY. Aculine, were you serious about getting together with Minerva?
ACULINE. Of course not. I was just toying with her to keep you two from tearin' hair. I haven't fooled around on Bernie since we've been together.

LILY. Oh, my cheeks hurt I'm so happy for you.
ACULINE. We've got a great thing goin'.
LILY. I sure wish I had your luck. My whole life people have wiped their feet on me like a door mat ... well, the "welcome" sign's finally worn off.
ACULINE. That's the spirit, child!
LILY. In fact, if Eddie Hyde were here right now ...

(*HYDE enters quietly, dressed as a policeman.*)

LILY. I'd fix his little red wagon.
ACULINE. Girl, there's not a mechanic on God's earth that could fix what's wrong with him.

(*THEY notice the policeman.*)

LILY. Officer! I told you about knocking before you come in.
HYDE. I just came by to get my little red wagon fixed. (*HE turns around.*)
LILY & ACULINE. Eddie!!!

(*THEY run as HE lunges towards them.*)

LILY. How did you get in here?!
HYDE. That unfortunate young patrolman out front was such a trusting soul. He didn't expect a fellow officer to knife him in the back.

(*HE pulls out a huge knife. ACULINE & LILY try to get away but they are cornered.*)

ACULINE. You killed a cop?
HYDE. Two, actually. The first was the fellow guarding my home. He didn't expect a killer to come from

within ... and his uniform fits me rather well, wouldn't you say?

ACULINE. Like a murderer's glove.

LILY. He was guarding *your* home?

HYDE. Yes. Doctor Jekyll and I share the same home.

ACULINE. So that's what's been getting into Doctor Jekyll's hide!

HYDE. I stay in the good doctor's laboratory. I find it most comfortable. You see, I was born in a scientific laboratory and spent most of my youth there.

ACULINE. And I bet you'd still be there if the apes hadn't taught you how to open your cage.

LILY. Henry's been hiding you? Then he told you what I said?

(Over the following ACULINE takes advantage of HYDE's attention to Lily and sneaks up behind him.)

HYDE. He didn't have to. I was so close I could hear you breathing. Just so you don't think ill of him, he did *try* to stop me. But as you can see, his efforts were as useless as trying to stop time by smashing a clock.

ACULINE. *(Jumps on Hyde's back.)* I got him! I got him! Woops! I don't got him no more!

(HE shakes her off and knocks her unconscious with his night stick.)

HYDE. So long, mama! Let's do the lunch thing sometime!

LILY. Aculine! Oh, my God! You've killed her!!!

HYDE. *(Throwing down the night stick.)* I doubt that I could have inflicted a blow hard enough to crack that thick skull of hers ... Now, why did you leave me?

LILY. I didn't have any choice!

HYDE. Yes, you did, my dear. You just made the wrong one.

LILY. I didn't have the sexual drive anymore.

HYDE. (*Throwing her to the floor.*) Perhaps you need another car!

LILY. (*Crawling away from him.*) Eddie, every time you touch me it's like feeling roaches between my clothes and my body.

HYDE. (*Takes a jar from his pocket and dumps its contents onto Lily.*) Excellent! The exact effect I try to cultivate.

(*Realizing Hyde has poured roaches onto her. LILY screams and frantically brushes them off.*)

HYDE. Now ... come to me, Lily ... one last time ...

(*SHE hits him in the groin as HE reaches for her. As HE bends over in pain SHE gets away from him. A chase ensues over the following.*)

HYDE. Don't get so excited! It's only a roll-in-the-hay not a walk on the moon.

LILY. The weirdest thing is, Eddie ... In a strange way I kinda liked you.

HYDE. That's the only way anybody can like me.

LILY. Your love of danger intoxicated me ... but you've got no feelings for anything else. If I kicked you in the heart, I'd break my leg.

(*HE finally catches her, throws her on the bed and begins to choke her.*)

LILY. Oh, hell! I give up! Go ahead and kill me.

HYDE. (*Lets go of her.*) Ah! The goodness within you beams from your kind face.

LILY. (*Confused.*) You have kind of a face too.

HYDE. You've lived for love and every time you've loved it's been your undoing.

LILY. Don't let these slits on my wrists fool ya.

HYDE. You should have picked yourself a man of character rather than characters pretending to be men.

LILY. Woulda, coulda, shoulda but didn't! So what?!!!

HYDE. Don't you want to try again, Lily? Don't you want happiness?

LILY. Everything I want seems to destroy something else I want. Go ahead! Do me a favor for once. Kill me!!!

(*SHE grabs his hands and puts them back around her neck. HE pulls away.*)

HYDE. No! Don't you see, you little fool? I want you to live.

LILY. Then you'd better leave, Eddie. The cops are gonna be hot on your tail and this is one of the first places they'll look.

HYDE. Yes. Yes ... But before I got I want to hear you say that you yearn to live in happiness!

LILY. But what if I fail?

HYDE. "In the bright lexicon of youth there is no such word as 'fail!' " And I'll bet you all the fleas in this place that Mr. Right is waiting for you out there somewhere.

LILY. You think so?

HYDE. Yeah! And, I'll bet your opera business really takes off too.

LILY. Yeah?

HYDE. Sure. You'll see. Charlie Chaplin wasn't the only tramp who could make it big.

LILY. You're just trying to be nice.

HYDE. When have I ever tried to be nice?
LILY. You've got a point.
HYDE. Sure. You've got a lot going for you, kid.
LILY. (*Smiles.*) Gee.
HYDE. Now, that's what I like to see. A big smile.
LILY. Eddie ... till now I thought you were total pond scum ... but you've given me the greatest gift in the world! Kiss me, Fate! I want to live!!! Thank you, Eddie! (*SHE embraces him and HE pulls away.*)
HYDE. "Gratitude is but a lame sentiment; thanks, when they are expressed, are often more embarrassing than welcome." I do have one last gift for you, Lily my dear. A necklace ... made of fingers!!! (*He begins to strangle her.*)
LILY. (*Choking.*) I thought you weren't going to kill me ...
HYDE. I lied.
LILY. (*Struggling to break free.*) Be a cannibal, Eddie! Eat a rat!!!
HYDE. That's right, Lily! Fight!
LILY. I trusted you.
HYDE. And I thank Satan you did. Once the trust goes out of a relationship, it's no fun lying anymore. You think I'd want to kill someone who *wanted* to die? That doesn't get my nuts off at all, angel cakes! (*HE lasciviously rubs against her while continuing to choke her.*)
LILY. You sick beast!
HYDE. "And the beasts shall reign over the earth!"
LILY. (*SHE is losing her strength. Barely audible.*) Please, Eddie. I can't breath ...
HYDE. "Was this the face that launched a thousand ships, and burnt the topless towers of Ilium? Sweet Helen, make me immortal with a kiss!"

(*HE kisses her as SHE goes totally limp, then holds up her lifeless body by the neck over the following.*)

HYDE. "Hell hath no limits, nor is circumscribed in one self place; for where we are is hell. And where hell is; there must we ever be."

(*HE lets go and Lily's body crumples to the floor just as BERNICE enters.*)

BERNICE. Oh, my God!
HYDE. (*Hisses like a cat.*) You're next, Doc!
BERNICE. (*Picks up Aculine's gun.*) Not if I can help it!

(*SHE shoots at him but HE escapes unharmed.*)

BERNICE. Damn! (*Trying to awaken Aculine.*) Honey! Honey, are you all right?
ACULINE. (*Coming around.*) Ohhh ... Bernie. I feel like I got hit over the head with a wet frying pan ... Oh! Lily! Where's Lily?
BERNICE. I don't think she was so lucky.
ACULINE. (*Sees Lily.*) Nooooo!!! Lily! Lily! ... Bernie! Go get that mother-fucker! I'll take care of this poor child ... He's probably headin' for the Jekyll place. He's been livin' in the laboratory.
BERNICE. Are you sure you'll be all right?
ACULINE. Just go, Bernie. But be careful. He killed the guards!
BERNICE. I wondered why no one was outside.
ACULINE. (*Screams.*) Will you just go!
BERNICE. Okay!

(*SHE runs out with the gun. ACULINE crawls over to Lily and weeps.*)

ACULINE. The poor little thing ... She never meant anybody harm ...

(*LIGHTS out.*)

ACT II

Scene 4

SCENE: Henry's laboratory moments later. HYDE enters with a paper take-out cup of coffee. HE changes his policeman's jacket for Henry's lab coat and quickly prepares the formula.

HYDE. Quickly, quickly! I must transform before anyone sees me. I've come to call you out, Henry my brother, a man who can afford to laugh at suspicion. In your impenetrable mantle of respect my safety is complete. You are a genius, Henry. But a short-sighted one. You never saw when you created me that I would become as strong as I have ... Intellectualism has bogged you down, brother.. Your mind is complex, where mine is simple and quick. We see the same things but our responses are totally different. Your first reaction is to think ... Mine is to act. For it is not just how we see, but how we perceive ... (*Finishes mixing the formula, HE toasts.*) Here's lookin' at you, kid!

(*BERNICE bursts into the room. Surprised, HYDE drops the formula/coffee. SHE aims the gun at him.*)

BERNICE. All right, Hyde! Hold it right there!

HYDE. (*Grabs his crotch.*) I'm holding. Now, what's up, Doc?

BERNICE. What have you done to Henry?

HYDE. Oh, he's around. But you'll never find him without my help.

BERNICE. Don't threaten me, you seditious savage! Why did you kill Lily?

HYDE. Because ... she didn't have what I'm lookin' for in a woman.

BERNICE. What's that ... break-away clothes?

HYDE. No. She had those. But beneath all that excites the eye, she was a simple girl with simple taste ... In short ... a bore. Fun is like insurance, Bernie baby. The older you get the more it costs. And let's face it ... she wasn't exactly what you'd call the higher priced spread.

BERNICE. You diseased animal!!!

HYDE. Ha ha ha ha ha ha ...

(*COCO jumps around in his cage as HYDE laughs. Suddenly HYDE is seized with pain. Then in Henry's voice.*)

HYDE. Bernice! Help me! Please!

BERNICE. That was Henry! Where is he, Hyde?! I'm warning you!

HYDE. You're warning me?! What do you know, woman? Go ahead! Shoot me and you'll never see your doctor friend again. (*HYDE jumps Bernice.*)

BERNICE. I'll save you, Henry!

(*THEY struggle and the gun goes off. HYDE is shot. BERNICE looks around.*)

BERNICE. Henry! Where are you?

HYDE. (*In Henry's voice.*) I'm here, Bernice!

BERNICE. What? If this is supposed to be funny ...

HYDE. (*In Henry's voice.*) Doctor Jekyll is *in* Mr. Hyde!

BERNICE. (*Grabs him by the collar.*) If Doctor Jekyll is Mr. Hyde then I'm Miss Seek!

HYDE. Agh! I'm not going to *lust* much longer! Ooooohhhhh ...

(*HYDE undergoes a total transformation, turning into Henry. BERNICE is seized with fright. As SHE watches the transformation her hair turns white.*)

BERNICE. My God! Oh, my God! Henry, I didn't know!

HENRY. There was no way you could know, my friend. I'm sorry for involving you. (*Notices her hair.*) Bernice! You've gone totally white with fright!

BERNICE. How did you ...

HENRY. I ingested the formula I discovered for my gold experiments. In doing so, I created in myself a model of the disease I wished to cure.

BERNICE. Quantum Synaptic Dualism?

HENRY. Yes, Bernice.

BERNICE. But, Henry. You knew the risks of such an experiment could far exceed the benefits ... Why?

HENRY. Vanity, Bernice. Pure and simple. It was the one trait Mr. Hyde and I shared ... But promise me, Bernice ... (*Coughs.*)

BERNICE. What is it, Henry?

HENRY. I'm dying ... destroy the formula and all records of these experiments.. (*Getting weaker.*) I've destroyed enough people's lives. I must save my dear Mary from all this ... Hurry, before the police get here ... The tapes and the computer discs ... They're all right there.

BERNICE. Yes, Henry. (*SHE packs some tapes and computer software into a briefcase, snaps it shut, and begins to cry.*) I'm so sorry, Henry.

(*HENRY tries to get up. BERNICE is surprised but helps him to his feet.*)

HENRY. It isn't your fault, Bernice. You acted to protect your friend. I wish I could have been a better friend to you.
BERNICE. Be still, Henry. You'll be fine. I'll go call an ambulance. (*SHE lets go of him and heads for the door.*)
HENRY. (*Falling to the floor.*) Wait! Vow to me, my friend, that the secret of Edward Hyde will never leave this place ... That like me, you will carry his secret to the grave.
BERNICE. I promise!
HENRY. Then Hyde will die here where he was born.

(*MARY and MINERVA enter.*)

MARY. Henry! (*Sees Bernice's white hair.*) What happened to you? ... Henry, what are you doing on the floor? (*SHE lets out a blood-curdling scream, scaring everyone including HENRY.*) I see blood!
HENRY. I've been shot, Mary my love.
MARY. Shot?!!! Who shot you?!!!
BERNICE. I ...
HENRY. Mr. Hyde shot me then escaped.
BERNICE. I ... I'll go call an ambulance.

(*SHE exits. HENRY begins coughing uncontrollably.*)

MINERVA. Henry! You're *really* hurt!
HENRY. I'm afraid so, Mary dear.

BERNICE. (*Enters.*) The medics are on their way.
HENRY. It's a little late for that, Bernice.

(*THEY do a slap-stick try-to-get-Henry-in-the-chair routine.*)

MARY. Where is this Hyde creature?
BERNICE. He killed Lily Gay then came here to get Henry.
MARY. He killed Lily Gay?! There go my opera lessons.
MINERVA. That's a shame.

(*LILY and ACULINE enter.*)

EVERYONE. Lily!!!
HENRY. Could this really be you, or have I died and gone to heaven?
LILY. (*Going to him.*) It's not heaven, Henry. I'm still here.
ACULINE. Bernie, your hair ...
BERNICE. Lily!
ACULINE. She passed out while Eddie was strangling her.
MINERVA. (*To Aculine.*) Say ... you look awfully familiar.
HENRY. Lily ... You don't know how happy it makes me that you're safe and well.
LILY. Gee, thanks, Doc. You're gonna be okay too. I just know it.
HENRY. In the next life perhaps ... but you still have this life which has so much to offer you.
MARY. Henry, why didn't you tell me about this Mr. Hyde?

HENRY. I know I should have told you ... and you would have understood. But at the time I thought it wiser not to expose you to the likes of such a monster ... The wisdom of one day is the folly of the next. (*HE appears to die then revives.*) How queer men are ...

(*EVERYONE does a take to the audience.*)

HENRY. They cannot detach themselves from their surrounds and criticize them. It is as if they were joined to the earth they stand on by the soles of their feet. Now that I shall never stand on my feet again, everything is clear to me. (*HE appears to die again.*)
MARY. Why did he want to kill you?
HENRY. (*Revives again.*) He saw me as a threat to his existence. He felt if I ceased to exist, he'd be free to live ... and he's won ... his secret will die with me ... But I too will be free ... (*Just as those seem to be his last words, HE rises from the chair, alarming EVERYONE.*)
Under the wide and starry sky,
Dig the grave and let me lie.
Glad did I live and gladly die,
And I laid me down with will ...
MARY. Oh, Henry!

(*HENRY finally dies. EVERYONE weeps as BERNICE continues the second stanza of Robert Louis Stevenson's* Requiem, *which is engraved on his tombstone.*)

BERNICE.
This be the verse you grave for me:
Here he lies where he longed to be;
Home is the sailor, home from the sea,
    And the hunter home from the hill .....

(*Suddenly the tragic tableau is broken by a flash of LIGHTNING, a clap of THUNDER, and a puff of SMOKE. MR. HYDE appears with a sickle in hand.*)

HYDE. Home is where the *horror* is!!!

(*EVERYONE screams with horror. LIGHTS out.*)

The End?

COSTUME PLOT

ACT I

<u>Scene 1-Living Room.</u>

MINERVA-A maid's uniform, black with white apron, white maid's cap, sensible black shoes, and flesh support hose. (*She wears this costume in all her scenes.*)

MARY-A gold and beige brocade, late 18th century-style house coat with gold underdress, and gold period slippers.

HENRY- A traditional style dark blue suit, dress shirt, tie, Oxford shoes, and wallet.

BERNICE-A tailored tweed skirt suit, medium heeled pumps, sheer hose, and a watch.

LILY-A short, white, fluffy crinoline skirt, tight black lace tank top, shiny black vinyl jacket, black lace knee-length hose laced up the back, high heels, and disco bag.

<u>Scene 2-Laboratory.</u>

HENRY-A crisp white lab coat over previous costume, minus suit jacket.

HYDE- Same costume as HENRY plus a spikey black wig which he wears in every scene.

<u>Scene 3-The Fruit Bowl.</u>

HYDE-A large, ill-fitting pin-stripe suit over a red, wide mesh fish net top with patches of long black hair sticking through it. Black pointy shoes, and black belt.

ACULINE- A tight yellow, low-cut, strapless cocktail dress with purple high heels.

LILY-1st Costume: A full-length, low-cut-, black velvet evening gown with puffy gold lamé sleeves, same hose as I-1, and gold lamé high heels.

2nd Costume: (*Quick change*) Tight gold sequin mini-skirt with wide purple velvet belt, yellow lycra tank top trimmed with black lace and sequins, and the same shoes and hose as I-3.

BERNICE-A tight dark skirt, purple t-shirt, black leather vest, and red mid-calf boots with medium heels.

Scene 4-LILLY's flat.

HYDE & LILY-Same as I-3

Scene 5-Living room.

MARY-1st Costume: Long Edwardian-style dress with high collar made of modern print fabric, and heels to match.

2nd Costume: Full-length African print kaftan, Afro wig, and sandals.

HENRY-Dark tween trousers, white shirt, colorful cardigan sweater,, tie, and Oxford shoes.

BERNICE-Tight black skirt, crepe blouse with bowed collar, and sensible shoes.

Scene 6-The Fruit Bowl.

LILY-Skin tight fades stretch jeans, "Girl Bar" t-shirt, and sling-back heels.

ACULINE-Colorful harem pants, sequin halter top, long silk chiffon scarf trimmed with sequins, and spike heels.

BERNICE-Same skirt as I-5, red mock turtle neck sweater, and same boots as I-3.

HYDE-Yellow polyester dinner jacket with black trim, black tuxedo trousers, white tux shirt, black bow tie, and same shoes as I-3.

Scene 7-A street corner.

HYDE-Same as I-6.

JEHOVAH'S WITNESS-Thick eyeglasses, 1970's style plaid polyester jacket, stiff polyester trousers, polyester shirt with wide collar, and nerdy brown shoes.

ACT II

Scene 1-Laboratory.

HENRY & HYDE. White lab coat, suit pants from I-1, white shirt, tie, Oxford shoes.

BERNICE-A different tight skirt, beige corporate blouse with red pin-stripes and sensible shoes.

Scene 2-Living room.

HYDE-Same as II-1.

MARY-A red plaid, floor length kilt, white blouse with puffed sleeves, huge Scottish sash worn over one shoulder, a fur trimmed tam hat, and bagpipes (optional).

LILY-A red skirt suit with low-cut, puffy sleeved top, and tight skirt. High heels with sheer hose.

ACULINE-A man's dark blue, double breasted, pin-striped suit, a white dress shirt, tie, fedora hat, and men's shoes.

HENRY-Same as II-1, but remove lab coat and add suit jacket from I-1.

MINERVA-Same costume, add 1950's style overcoat and hat for her last exit.

Scene 3-LILY's flat.

ACULINE-Trousers, shirt and socks from II-2 with a bright orange 1940's floral print house coat.

LILY- (*Quick change, worn under last costume.*) Same top as I-1 with 4 gold buttons velcroed down the front, a tight black knit mini-skirt/slip with cut out lace panels up the sides. A black lacy negligée is worn over this.

HYDE-A policeman's uniform with cap and nightstick.

BERNICE-A tailored olive skirt suit, and sensible pumps.

Scene 4-Laboratory.

HYDE & HENRY-Same as II-3, plus lab coat.

BERNICE-Same as II-3.

MARY-Another contemporary version of an Edwardian dress, with shoes to match.
LILY-Same as II-3, plus jacket from I-1, a purple chiffon neck scarf, and high heels.
ACULINE-Same as II-3, minus house coat, plus a hand-painted denim jacket.

Jewelry
MARY-Pearls and Victorian cameos, etc.
LILY-Hearts and stars, bangle bracelets.
ACULINE-Bangles and large cut stones.
BERNICE-A watch, simple earrings, and a phone beeper.
MINERVA-Simple clip-on earrings.

Hairstyles
LILY & ACULINE's hairstyles are 50's/60's retro, very "girl-group" bubbles and beehives. MARY's hair is worn like different styles from periods of the 19th century. MINERVA's hair is sort of a frumpy page boy, and BERNICE has a very butch men's 50's flat-top.

PROPERTY LIST

ACT I

On side table in living room:
- telephone
- note pad & pencil

- postage stamp

MARY brings on:
- matchbook
- envelope
- newspaper ("the Coxsackie Tatler") with headlines reading "Secret Psycho Seized"

Doorbell

Coffee service brought on by MINERVA:
- tray
- coffee pot
- creamer
- sugar bowl
- 4 cups & saucers
- teaspoons

MINERVA's brings on:
- Small tray with sandwich and coffee cup

COCO the monkey could be a puppet (like in the original production) or an actor in costume

On lab table:
- beaker
- chemistry set up (real of part of a painted set)
- test tube
- sm. audio cassette recorder
- golden bowl
- sm. paint brush

Computer (painted or real)

Chalk board
Chalk
Chalk board eraser

HENRY's wallet with:
- calling card
- paper money

feather duster
Rubber frog
MARY's audio cassette player with headphones
blank pistol with leg holster & blanks
champagne cork
sandwich board for Jehovah's Witness
2 champagne glasses
pair of handcuffs

On LILY's bed:
-brassiere
-panties
On LILY's table:
-sheet music
Mail: 3 bills; junk mail;
manila envelope
   containing:
-audio cassette tape
-*AIDA* libretto
-personal letter
-Afro wig

4 highball glasses
Double shot glass
-dildo
Microphone with stand

ACT II

MARY carries on:
-tray of sandwiches
-tray of cakes

MINERVA carries on:
-coffee service (as before)
LILY's large audio cassette
   player with shoulder
   strap

ACULINE carries 3 "Lucia
   de Lammermoor"
   librettos
ice pack for the head

LILY's pitchpipe

policeman's nightstick
   (plastic)
HYDE's sm. plastic jar
   filled with rubber
   cockroaches
white wig styled like
   Bernice's hair

large stage knife

HYDE's sm. paper bag
   with take-out cup of
   coffee
newspaper headlined:
   "Crime Wave Rocks
   Coxsackie"

In or on lab table:
-audio tapes
-briefcase
-sickle

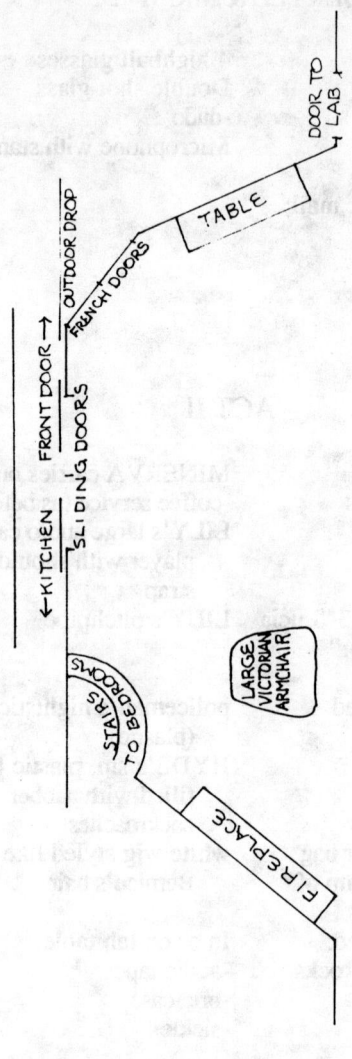

LIVING ROOM I-1&5, II-2

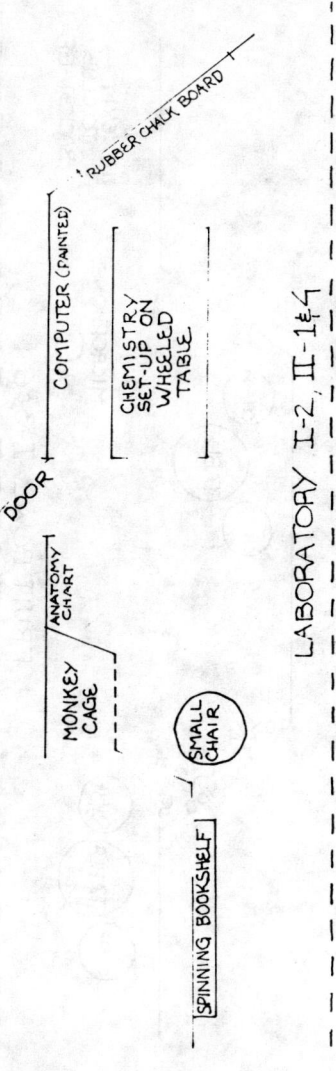

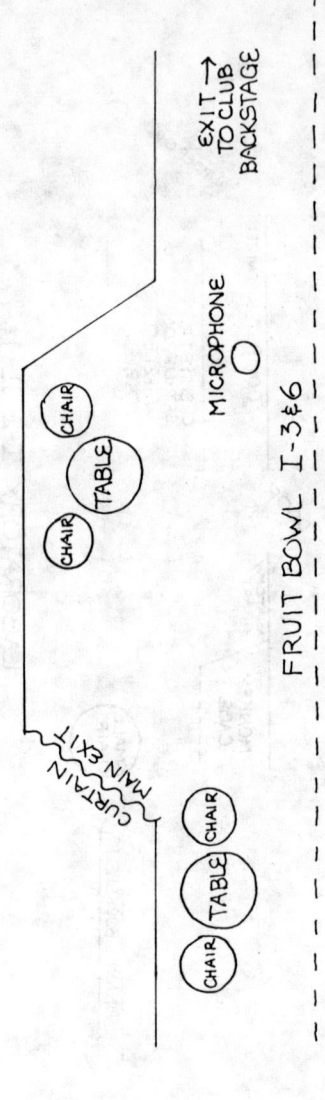

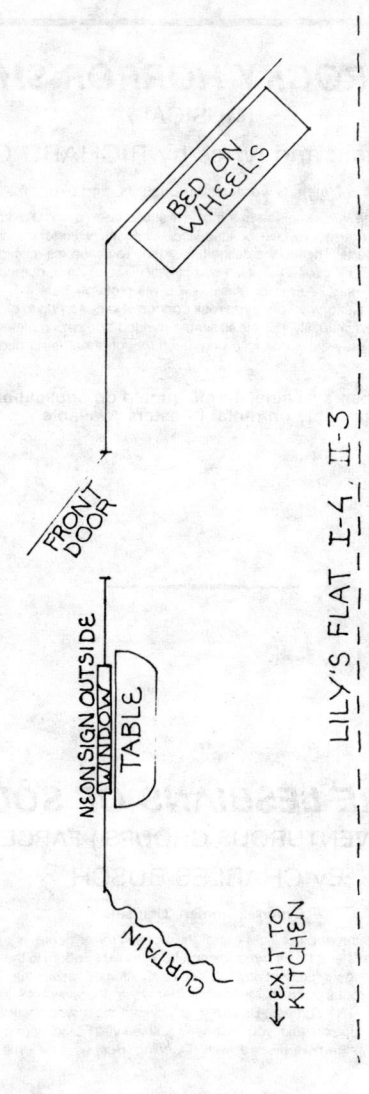

Other Publications for Your Interest

THE ROCKY HORROR SHOW
(MUSICAL)
Book, music and lyrics by RICHARD O'BRIEN

7 men, 3 women. Various ints. and exts.

At last! The original stage version of the cult movie that has been a "12 O'clock high" for thousands of enthusiastic movie-goers. Live, on stage, see Dr. Frank N. Furter match wits (?) with the innocent young newlyweds! Thrill to the delightfully trashy rock and roll music! "It isn't a play, it isn't a musical, it isn't a rock concert... It's a sort of glitter, rock, horror, comedy, tranvestite circus... And if you love—say, 'Sound of Music'—you will probably hate it."—WABC-TV. "*The Rocky Horror Show* is a sicko-wacko-weirdo rock concert. It keeps trying to blow your mind with loud music and perverted sexuality, but it is so simple-minded, and so completely silly, that it ends up being a lot of fun. It may get a cult following, even though there is no nudity."—NBC.

(#20049)

(Restricted. When available, Terms quoted on application—Music available on rental.) Posters Available

VAMPIRE LESBIANS OF SODOM
(ADVENTUROUS GROUPS.) FARCE
By CHARLES BUSCH

6 men, 2 women. Unit set

This truly bizarre entertainment, cut right out of the *Rocky Horror* genre, is about vamps, has nothing to do with lesbians and takes the audience from ancient Sodom to the Hollywood of the twenties, ending up somehow in present day Las Vegas. "Costumes flashier than pinball machines, outrageous lines, awful puns, sinister innocence, harmless depravity—it's all here. One can imagine a cult forming."—NY Times. "Bizarre and wonderful... If you think Boy George is a gender-bender, well, like Jolson said, you ain't seen nothing yet! Forget your genders, come on, get happy."—Broadway Mag. Published with *Sleeping Beauty*, or *Coma*. (Royalty, $50-$40.)

(#24006).